Life & Times in 20th-Century America

Volume 4: Troubled Times at Home

1961–1980

Greenwood Publishing Group

Library of Congress Cataloging-in-Publication Data
Life & times in 20th-century America / by Media Projects, Inc.
     p. cm
     Includes bibliographical references and indexes.
  Contents: v. 1. Becoming a modern nation, 1900-1920 — v. 2. Boom times, hard times,
1921-1940 — v. 3. Hot and cold wars, 1941-1960 — v. 4. Troubled times at home,
1961-1980 — v. 5. Promise and change, 1981-2000.
  ISBN 0–313–32570–7 (set: alk. paper)—ISBN 0–313–32571–5 (v. 1: alk. paper) —
ISBN 0–313–32572–3 (v. 2: alk. paper)—ISBN 0–313–32573–1 (v. 3: alk. paper) —
ISBN 0–313-32574–X (v. 4: alk. paper)—ISBN 0–313–32575–8 (v. 5: alk. paper)
  1. United States—History—20th century. 2. United States—Social conditions—20th
century. 3. United States—Social life and customs—20th century. I. Media Projects
Incorporated.
E741.L497 2004
973.91—dc21   2003044829

British Library Cataloguing in Publication Data is available.
Copyright © 2004 by Greenwood Publishing Group, Inc.

Library of Congress Catalog Card Number: 2003044829
ISBN: 0–313–32570–7 (set)
     0–313–32571–5 (vol. 1)
     0–313–32572–3 (vol. 2)
     0–313–32573–1 (vol. 3)
     0–313–32574–X (vol. 4)
     0–313–32575–8 (vol. 5)

First published in 2004

Greenwood Press, 88 Post Road West, Westport, CT 06881
An imprint of Greenwood Publishing Group, Inc.
www.greenwood.com

Printed in the United States of America

The paper used in this book complies with the
Permanent Paper Standard issued by the National
Information Standards Organization (Z39.48–1984).

10 9 8 7 6 5 4 3 2 1

Media Projects, Inc.
Managing Editor: Carter Smith
Editor: Carolyn Jackson
Writer: Stuart Murray
Production Editor: Jim Burmester
Indexer: Marilyn Flaig
Designer: Amy Henderson
Copy Editor: Elin Woodger

Contents

A "New Frontier" and Old Challenges

"Ask not what your country can do for you—ask what you can do for your country."

With this challenge, John F. Kennedy took office as the thirty-fifth president of the United States. These words were part of President Kennedy's inaugural address on January 20, 1961, as he asked the next generations of Americans—those who had grown up during World War II (1939–1945) and their children—to serve the country unselfishly.

Kennedy declared, "We stand on the edge of a 'New Frontier,'" for the American frontier was no longer defined by new lands or wilderness to conquer, but by the need for improvements to society. Many of Kennedy's policies as president would be known as New Frontier programs.

A Massachusetts senator and a Democrat, Kennedy only narrowly defeated Republican vice president Richard M. Nixon in 1960 by 118,550 votes out of 86.3 million cast. Kennedy soon won broad popular support, however, bringing a spirit of optimism to America. That optimism was, in part, thanks to the personal charm of this handsome young president and his beautiful wife, Jacqueline Bouvier Kennedy. At forty-three, JFK, as he was often tagged, was the youngest president ever. He was also the first Catholic elected to lead the nation.

The United States was still engaged with the communist Union of Soviet Socialist Republics (USSR) in a Cold War rivalry that had been played out around the world since World War II ended in 1945. Although the two nations had united in defeating Germany, Italy, and Japan, they were now bitter rivals. Each sought to win over other, neutral nations, such as India and Egypt, to their way of governing and managing an economy. In

CLOCKWISE: **Two young women attend a music festival.** (Archive Photos); **John F. Kennedy** (Library of Congress); **American troops in Vietnam.** (National Archives)

President Kennedy with his wife Jackie, son John, Jr., and daughter Caroline (Library of Congress)

the United States, leaders were chosen through democratic elections, and wealth and property were privately held. In the Soviet Union, the Communist Party ruled with an iron hand and held all property and wealth in the name of the people.

During the first year of his presidency, Kennedy faced dramatic and dangerous international situations. Among these was a failed invasion of the island of Cuba. That island, just ninety miles from the Florida coast, had come under communist control in 1959. In April 1961, 1,200 anti-communist Cubans, trained and equipped by the U.S. Central Intelligence Agency (CIA), invaded Cuba but failed to oust its dictator, Fidel Castro. Kennedy was blamed for this defeat. Even though the operation had been planned during the administration of the previous president, Dwight D. Eisenhower, Kennedy accepted responsibility.

1961

John F. Kennedy of Massachusetts is inaugurated as president after defeating Vice President Richard Nixon of California the previous fall.

1961

U.S.-trained anti-communist Cubans invade Cuba, landing at the Bay of Pigs. The invasion fails.

The Soviet Union divides Berlin by building a wall to keep citizens from escaping.

1963

Civil rights leader Martin Luther King, Jr., leads a march on Washington, D.C., to demand equal rights for African Americans. At the end of the march, he gives his famous "I Have A Dream" speech.

1963

President Kennedy is assassinated while visiting Dallas, Texas. Vice President Lyndon Johnson of Texas becomes president.

A few months later, in October 1961, Soviet-built nuclear missile bases were discovered in Cuba. President Kennedy strongly warned Soviet leader Nikita Khrushchev that the United States might attack if the missiles were not dismantled. For two weeks, the Soviets and Americans faced off, and some feared nuclear war was at hand. The world waited breathlessly until Khrushchev at last backed off and agreed to remove the missiles.

The Kennedy presidency came to a sudden and shocking end in Dallas, Texas, on November 22, 1963, when JFK was assassinated by a sniper. The entire world mourned Kennedy's death. It seemed a certain American innocence had been lost.

Vice President Lyndon B. Johnson, often called LBJ, succeeded JFK to become the thirty-sixth president of the United States.

Peace Corps Volunteers and Civil Rights Activists

Since the end of World War II, many countries had become independent of their old colonial rulers. Most of them, such as those in Africa and Latin America, had little industry. European nations that controlled them as colonies had taken mostly raw materials like oil, rubber, gold and other resources from them without developing their local economies. The New Frontier policies of the Kennedy administration were started to help the people build up poor countries.

One of the most popular groups started at this time was the Peace

1964

The British rock group The Beatles arrive in the United States for the first time.

President Lyndon Johnson defeats Senator Barry Goldwater of Arizona to win election as president.

1964

The United States begins sending troops to South Vietnam to aid that country against communist rebels.

1967

President Johnson nominates Thurgood Marshall for the Supreme Court. Marshall becomes the first African American to serve on the Court.

1968

President Johnson announces that he will not run for reelection.

Martin Luther King, Jr., is assassinated.

Dr. Martin Luther King, Jr.
(Library of Congress)

Corps. It sent thousands of American volunteers to poor countries. There they taught farming techniques, showed how to build water and sewage systems, and started new health and educational programs. Peace Corps volunteers learned the local language and lived with the host people on equal terms. Volunteers eventually served in more than sixty countries.

President Kennedy also worked to create new civil rights laws at home, but conservative southern Democrats and Republicans in Congress refused to support him because they thought the federal government took too much power from the states. Massive marches on Washington, D.C., by hundreds of thousands of civil rights activists riveted national attention. Still, the popular mood, especially in the South, did not favor full civil rights for African Americans. Congress failed to pass new civil rights bills during the Kennedy administration. However, Kennedy did attempt to enforce existing laws.

Leading the administration's civil rights policies was one of JFK's two younger brothers: Robert, the attorney general. Bobby Kennedy, as he was

1968

Senator Robert F. Kennedy, younger brother of President John F. Kennedy and leading candidate for the Democratic nomination for president, is assassinated.

1968

Former Vice President Richard Nixon defeats Vice President Hubert Humphrey to become president.

1969

Apollo astronauts Neil Armstrong and Edwin "Buzz" Aldrin become the first two men to walk on the moon.

More than 300,000 young people attend the Woodstock rock festival.

1971

More than 250,000 Americans arrive in Washington, D.C., to protest the war in Vietnam.

often called, worked to protect civil rights activists and demonstrators in the South. In one situation, he sent 400 U.S. marshals to Montgomery, Alabama, to protect Dr. Martin Luther King, Jr., the Civil Rights movement's most famous leader, against a hostile mob.

At a civil rights march on Washington in August 1963, King stood before the Lincoln Memorial and gave a memorable public address, known as the "I Have a Dream" speech. He said it was his dream that one day all men would be brothers and that his children would not be judged by their skin color but by their character. King won the Nobel Peace Prize the next year.

Equal rights between the sexes and discrimination against women also became important subjects of discussion and controversy. What became known as the women's liberation movement began to take shape. In 1963, President Kennedy established the Presidential Commission on the Status of Women, which studied the place of women in society. Author Betty Friedan published *The Feminine Mystique*, a book that encouraged women to build identities for themselves outside the home.

The Youth Movement

The 1960s were also a time of change for America's young people. As the decade opened, many of them were inspired by President Kennedy's call to give back to the nation and the world. Thousands of recent college graduates volunteered for the Peace Corps.

1972

The United States and Soviet Union sign the Strategic Arms Limitation Treaty (SALT), a treaty to limit the spread of nuclear weapons.

1972

President Nixon approves a break-in at the Democratic Party headquarters in Washington, D.C.'s Watergate Hotel.

President Nixon defeats Senator George McGovern of South Dakota to win reelection.

1973

After the United States backs Israel in a war against Egypt and Syria, the Arab-led Organization of Petroleum Exporting Countries (OPEC) cuts oil sales to the United States, Europe, and Japan. The cut causes an energy shortage in the United States and elsewhere.

1973

The United States and North Vietnam sign a peace treaty in Paris, France, ending the United States' involvement in the Vietnam War. The next year, South Vietnam is taken over by the communists.

While many young people were inspired by Kennedy's words, some also began to question whether America always lived up to the ideals of justice and equality for all Americans. Many young people of all races were inspired by Dr. Martin Luther King and his fellow civil rights activists in the South as they fought for desegregation, voting rights, and respect. Thousands of young people—many of them still in college—helped organize voter registration drives across the South. (Although African Americans were legally allowed to vote, most were prevented from voting by local government laws such as "poll taxes" and literacy tests that made voting more difficult for poor African Americans. African Americans who dared to vote also risked violence from hate groups such as the Ku Klux Klan.)

Despite the potential danger, many young people tried to change things for the better. The summer of 1964, for instance, was known as "Freedom Summer," as white and black students from around the nation headed south to Mississippi, Alabama, and other segregated states to help African Americans register to vote. After civil rights protesters in Selma, Alabama were beaten by police in early 1965 while trying to hold a protest march for voting rights, many young people joined a second, larger march from that city to Alabama's capital of Montgomery. A few months later, the federal government passed a new national law. The Voting Rights Act of 1965 made it illegal to prevent someone from voting due to their race.

1973

The U.S. Supreme Court legalizes abortion in the case of *Roe v. Wade*.

1974

President Nixon is forced to resign from office after investigations show that the Watergate break-in was part of a larger illegal operation and that the president had lied to cover it up. Vice President Gerald Ford becomes president.

1974

President Ford pardons Richard Nixon for any crimes that he may have committed in office.

1976

The United States celebrates its bicentennial, or 200th anniversary.

Georgia governor Jimmy Carter defeats Gerald Ford to become president.

Changing Times

The Civil Rights movement helped many young people feel that they could make the world a better place. Many felt they needed to speak out when they believed the older generation was wrong. For example, one of the young people who traveled to the South to support the Civil Rights movement was a folksinger named Bob Dylan. In his song "The Times They Are A-Changin'" he wrote, "Come mothers and fathers throughout the land . . . don't criticize what you can't understand. . . . Your sons and your daughters are beyond your command. . . ." The song became an anthem of the protest movement. It also expressed the idea that young people would shape their lives for themselves, even if their parents did not approve.This attitude influenced more than the protest movement. It also helped shape other areas of society, including music, fashion, art, and more.

In 1964, the British rock group, The Beatles—John Lennon, Paul McCartney, George Harrison, and Ringo Starr—arrived in the United States. Although the group would disband six years later, they would change the face of popular music. With their success, a "British Invasion" of rock groups, including the Rolling Stones, the Animals, and the Who, also found success in the United States.

Like Bob Dylan, The Beatles and other British-invasion groups also influenced popular culture. Millions of fans followed along as their favorite stars grew their hair longer and began dressing more flamboyantly.

1978
President Carter helps to negotiate peace between Israel and Egypt.

1979
A mechanical failure triggers the worst radiation leak in the history of American nuclear power.

1979
After the shah of Iran is overthrown, Iranian revolutionaries capture the U.S. embassy in Tehran, Iran's capital. Fifty-three Americans are taken hostage.

1980
Ronald Reagan, former governor of California, defeats President Jimmy Carter to become president.

By the late 1960s, the spirit of experimentation led some young people, known as hippies, to even more unusual fashion. Piecing together mix and match outfits from second-hand clothing stores, attics, and boutiques, these youth took to wearing such clothing as fringed jackets, cowboy boots, bell-bottomed blue jeans, tie-dyed shirts, army fatigues, flowing dresses and blouses, and anything else that fit the mood of the day. These clothes were often accompanied by beaded necklaces, flowers in the hair, and peace sign decals.

The Vietnam War and LBJ

Since the mid-1950s, American foreign policy had opposed communist expansion in Southeast Asia, also known as Indochina. That Southeast Asian region included the new nations of North Vietnam and South Vietnam as well as Laos, Thailand, Cambodia, and Burma. These countries had been created in 1954 after the Vietnamese defeated the French, who had held Indochina as a colony before Japan had seized control of the area during World War II.

North Vietnam came under the control of local communists, while South Vietnam was a democratic republic ruled by an elected president. But South Vietnamese officials were often corrupt and harshly put down any opposition. This created deep hostility among many Vietnamese, who rebelled against the government. By the first years of the 1960s, civil strife and violence was tearing South Vietnam apart. North Vietnam supported rebels known as the Viet Cong. The United States supported the South Vietnamese government, supplying it with weapons and training its troops.

The American military was unhappy that the South Vietnamese could not defeat the Viet Cong. In 1963, the United States secretly supported a military coup, or overthrow, against the South Vietnamese president, who was assassinated. A new leader favorable to the Americans was installed.

In 1964, the U.S. military accused North Vietnamese torpedo boats of attacking American navy vessels in the Gulf of Tonkin off of the Vietnamese coast. Years later, this accusation would be proven false, but in 1964 it angered Americans. Congress passed the Gulf of Tonkin Resolution to authorize the use of troops in Vietnam. Lyndon Johnson was reelected president in November 1964, defeating Republican Barry Goldwater by a landslide—43.1 million votes to 27.1 million. Goldwater had proposed fighting the war more vigorously, while Johnson promised not to extend it. Nevertheless, within a year, 75,000 American troops were in South Vietnam fighting alongside South Vietnam's government forces.

By 1967, the United States had assumed leadership of the war. Soon there would be more than 500,000 U.S. troops in Indochina. As casualties mounted and the war's end seemed nowhere in sight, opposition to the war grew steadily in the United States. Millions of young men were drafted into military service, but those who remained in college making good grades were exempt, or temporarily excused, from the draft. This created class tensions. Those who could not afford to go to college had no protection against the draft.

The Vietnam War divided the United States between those who were pro-war ("hawks") and those who were antiwar ("doves"). Families, communities, universities, and colleges suffered deep and painful differences that created a lasting bitterness on both sides. Men who opposed the war often refused to be drafted. As a result, some of these "draft dodgers" were imprisoned. Others moved to Canada. Massive antiwar demonstrations were held around the country.

1968: A Terrible Year

The United States was in turmoil in 1968. In March, under severe criticism for escalating, or stepping up, the war, President Johnson announced that he would not seek another term. Before leaving office, however, he started peace talks with the North Vietnamese.

In April, Dr. Martin Luther King, Jr., was shot and killed by a sniper while organizing workers in Memphis, Tennessee. King's alleged assassin, James Earl Ray, was apprehended and later confessed. Social unrest deepened, and riots erupted among black communities. National Guard troops were called in to quell the disturbances. Still, scores of civilians were killed, thousands injured, and property damage was in the many millions of dollars. Largely white-owned commercial districts in African American neighborhoods were looted and burned to the ground.

In June, Senator Robert Kennedy, who might have been the Democrat-

Lyndon Johnson (Library of Congress)

ic Party's first choice as a presidential candidate, was assassinated during a political tour in Los Angeles. An assassin, Sirhan Sirhan, was captured on the scene, tried, and imprisoned. Government investigations did not attribute either the Kennedy or the King assassinations to any wider conspiracy.

LBJ's Great Society

Although the country had become bogged down in Vietnam under President Johnson's leadership, his administration had made great social progress at home. Its "war on poverty" and landmark civil rights legislation were its biggest achievements.

Building on JFK's ideal of a New Frontier, LBJ named his vision of America the "Great Society." Congress and the administration took new steps to address poverty, improve housing and mass transportation, rebuild inner cities, and aid the elderly. After his landslide victory over Goldwater in 1964, Johnson's popularity with voters and his influence in Congress also gave him the power to establish Medicare, a program that helps senior citizens pay for medical and hospital care, and nursing-home care for the aged.

In the middle of the 1960s, urban African American communities rioted against unequal job opportunities and poor housing. Johnson set up a commission to investigate the riots. The resulting report called for state and federal governments to provide improved housing, better education, and more police for the inner cities.

Missions to the Moon and Beyond

On April 12, 1961, the Soviet Union became the first country to launch a man into outer space when Yuri Gagarin circled the earth in space—traveling 24,600 miles. Although Alan Shepard, Jr., became the first American in space a month later, his 15-minute flight took him only 300 miles.

After Shepard's flight, President Kennedy made a dramatic promise. He

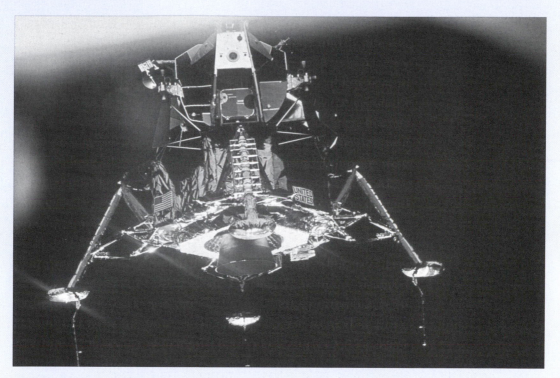

Apollo 11's **lunar landing module, the *Eagle*, heads for the moon.** (National Aeronautics and Space Administration)

announced to the world that before the 1960s were over, the National Aeronautics and Space Administration (NASA) would land a man on the moon and return him to earth. Before his death in 1963, Kennedy saw astronaut John Glenn become the first American to orbit the earth.

Just as Lyndon Johnson had built on President Kennedy's goal of a "New Frontier," he also helped follow through on JFK's mission to the moon. During Johnson's time in office, the United States moved closer and closer to a moon landing. In 1965, Edward White became the first American to walk in space. Sadly, in 1967, the U.S. space program suffered a tragedy when an electrical fire killed Edward White and two other astronauts during a training exercise.

On July 16, 1969, however, tragedy turned to triumph for the astronauts of the *Apollo 11* mission. While astronaut Michael Collins orbited the moon in the command ship *Columbia*, astronauts Neil Armstrong and Edwin "Buzz" Aldrin guided the lunar landing craft *Eagle* onto the surface of the moon. Stepping onto the moon's surface, Armstrong radioed back to earth, "That's one small step for man, one giant leap for mankind."

Richard Nixon (Library of Congress)

Over the next several years, more American missions landed on the moon. In 1973, *Skylab*, a 118-foot long orbiting space station was launched. The purpose of *Skylab* was to increase knowledge of space, to study the effects of weightlessness on humans, and to monitor the earth's ability to support its population.

During the late 1960s and the 1970s, NASA also launched several series of dramatic unmanned space flights. Satellites in the Mariner program photographed Venus and Mars, while the Viking program actually landed mechanical probes on Mars's surface. In one exciting discovery, the first *Viking* probe discovered water in Mars's soil. Finally, the Pioneer missions explored Venus as well as the outer planets of the solar system, such as Jupiter and Saturn.

Nixon's War in Vietnam

In the November 1968 presidential election, Republican Richard M. Nixon narrowly defeated Hubert H. Humphrey in the popular vote—31.8 million votes to 31.3 million—winning election as the thirty-seventh president.

Although he was a longtime, hard-hitting anticommunist, Nixon had campaigned on a promise to end the Vietnam War. He began a gradual withdrawal of American troops from Vietnam but at the same time secretly widened the war. In 1970, these secret wars were made public, and another round of antiwar demonstrations began.

Some demonstrations involved violence. The most tragic was a clash between demonstrators and National Guard troops at Kent State University in Ohio. The little-trained guardsmen fired at random toward a crowd of demonstrators, killing four students and wounding others, some of them merely passersby.

Protesters outside the White House call for President Nixon to resign. (Library of Congress)

Reelection and Resignation

Although the American economy stumbled and weakened, Nixon remained popular with voters in the 1972 presidential election. He won easily over Democrat George S. McGovern of South Dakota, who favored an immediate end to the war and a return to domestic programs like those favored by former presidents Kennedy and Johnson. Nixon won reelection by 47.1 million votes to 29.1 million.

During the campaign, however, Republican agents on a spying mission broke into the Democratic Party's national headquarters. Police caught the intruders, and thus began the Watergate scandal, so named after the Washington office-apartment complex that housed the headquarters.

Congress increased pressure on Nixon to provide more information about what he knew of the Watergate burglary. When it was revealed that he had secretly taped conversations in the presidential office, Congress asked for the tapes, and he refused. When consulted, the Supreme Court ruled unanimously that the tapes should be turned over. Meanwhile, the Senate judiciary committee voted to impeach the president on the grounds that he had obstructed justice. He was accused of paying hush money to witnesses, withholding evidence, and using the CIA, FBI, and Internal Revenue Service to deprive Americans of constitutional rights to privacy and free speech. Soon afterward, on August 9, 1974, Nixon resigned as president, the first ever to do so. He was succeeded by Vice President Ford, who became the thirty-eighth president.

Economic Woes

As the nation struggled to pay for the Vietnam War in the midst of a slowing economy, the 1970s were plagued by inflation (or rising prices) and high unemployment. The war had wiped out the surplus money in the federal treasury that had been piling up since World War II. By 1974, there was a $500 billion national debt. While Watergate riveted the nation's attention, prices for food and oil skyrocketed.

The Nixon administration had tried to deal with inflation by placing controls on workers' wages and the prices of American goods and services. At the same time, it taxed products, such as automobiles, imported from other nations. This was unsuccessful since it made these products more expensive. During 1974 and 1975, car sales fell by 35 percent. During the same period, the construction of new homes fell 40 percent, and a record 120,000 Americans declared personal bankruptcy. President Ford would have to deal with the worst economic recession, or downturn, since the Great Depression.

Gerald Ford (Library of Congress)

The Ford Administration

As an appointed vice president, Gerald Ford was the first president not elected to either the presidency or the vice presidency. In the wake of Nixon's resignation, Ford assured Americans in his inaugural address: "Our long national nightmare is over."

A month later, Ford granted a full pardon to Nixon. This guaranteed that the former president could not be charged with any crime related to his time in office. Many Americans who had been comforted by the president's earlier assurance were now outraged. When Congress held investigations to determine if the new president had made a deal with the old one—the presidency for a pardon—it found no evidence. However, for many the pardon again raised the issue of whether or not presidents are above the law, and Ford's reputation suffered.

President Ford quickly addressed his economic dilemma. He championed free markets (or little government involvement in the economy). He rejected Nixon-era wage and price controls and import taxes. Instead, Ford cut federal spending and asked for a tax on corporations and wealthy people, which Congress passed. In addition, he launched a public campaign called "Whip Inflation Now," or "WIN." Hundreds of thousands of metal WIN buttons were produced, but there was little ordinary people could do to stop inflation. It remained stuck at 11 percent. In January 1975, Ford reversed course and called for a tax cut on businesses, which Congress passed. Inflation slowed, but it was still a problem. The difference between government spending and government income created a deficit that continued to rise.

A high point of the Ford presidency was the nation's celebration of its bicentennial in 1976. The Fourth of July was the 200th anniversary of the signing of the Declaration of Independence. Events, projects, and commemorations were held all over the country in a year-long national festival.

Carter Takes Office

Former Georgia governor Jimmy Carter, a Democrat, was elected president in 1976, defeating President Ford. The popular vote was 40.8 million for Carter to Ford's 39.1 million.

As the thirty-ninth president, Carter brought a new idealism to the White House. Carter's idealism and zeal for reform often infuriated people. Some felt that as an outsider to Washington, he lacked the proper respect for the way things were done.

Carter's most outstanding foreign-policy success was to bring the leaders of Israel and Egypt, bitter enemies, to a summit meeting at Camp David in Maryland, in 1978. There, terms were established with Israeli prime minister Menachem Begin and Egyptian president Anwar Sadat for a peace treaty that was signed the following year. (Although Begin and Sadat won the

Jimmy Carter (Library of Congress)

Nobel Peace Prize for this achievement, Sadat was later assassinated in his own country. The Nobel Prize would not be given to Carter until 2002.)

Protecting the Environment

During the 1960s and 1970s, many Americans began to worry about the harm that pollution was doing to the environment. In 1962, biologist Rachel Carson published her book *Silent Spring*. The book detailed what she saw as the dangers of chemical pesticides. In 1970, an estimated 20 million Americans participated in the first Earth Day celebration. Some marched in parades to promote cleaner air and water, others organized litter clean-ups and others gathered at the Washington, D.C. mall to hear speakers and rock music.

In response to this public demand for a cleaner environment, many new laws were written during the 1970s. The Clean Water Act and the Clean Air Act, both passed by Congress in 1970, came during President Nixon's first term in office. The same year, Congress also set up the Environmental Protection Agency, a government department in charge of enforcing environmental laws.

Not all environmental proposals were passed, however. President Carter tried to establish federal policies to conserve natural resources and protect the environment. He called for energy programs to reduce the country's dependence on foreign oil and promote alternative fuels and energy sources. But Congress and the business community would not support him.

"The Me Decade"

During the 1960s, the civil rights and antiwar movements inspired many Americans to try to improve the world, but by the 1970s, many people began looking for new ways to improve themselves. By the middle of the decade, writer Tom Wolfe had begun calling the 1970s, "the Me Decade," and the term stuck.

For some, self-improvement meant taking up jogging, or joining a fitness or diet club. Others took up health food, eating brown rice, tofu, alfalfa sprouts, and even seaweed.

Another self-improvement trend involved new forms of spirituality and therapy. Many began exploring yoga or forms of Eastern religions, such as meditation. Still others tried unusual forms of therapy, such as "primal scream therapy," which involved letting go of hidden anger through screaming. Another popular trend was called "est," which stood for Erhard Seminars Training, after the group's founder, a former used-car salesman Werner Erhard.

At the same time, many Americans found a more traditional route to self-improvement during the 1970s. By 1977, 70 million Americans—including President Carter and country singer Johnny Cash—identified themselves as "born-again Christians." By the end of the decade, the growth of born-again Christianity had allowed the Virginia-based Christian Broadcast Network (CBN) to blossom into a powerful media company with four television stations and annual revenues of $60 million a year. During the 1980s and 1990s, the station grew even faster. The company's founder, Reverend Pat Robertson, would even run for president.

Some trends of the 1970s had little to do with self-improvement. They simply were fun. By the middle of the decade, a new music style called disco became popular. Based on funky beats and propulsive rhythms, disco brought with it new dance crazes such as "The Hustle." It also provided the soundtrack for one of the decades most popular movies, *Saturday Night Fever*.

Both the 1960s and 1970s were times of enormous change and conflict. Americans lived through assassinations, battles over civil rights, the Vietnam War, and the Watergate scandal. As they did, they spoke out for change, experimented with a new lifestyles, fashions, and fads. By 1980, the mood of the country had changed. Many Americans wanted to get return to simpler times and more straightforward, old-fashioned values. Although many of the attitudes of the 1960s and 1970s would be abandoned in the 1980s and 1990s, the next decades would not prove to be any simpler than the ones that had just ended.

Chapter One

Family Life

By the early 1960s, the foundations of American life were being shaken by troubles on the world scene and at home. The oldest baby boomers were growing up, and many found the stable home life they had always known was falling apart. In the next twenty years, the unity of both the nation and the family would be severely tested.

Internationally, the greatest trouble was in distant Vietnam, where the United States went to war. The federal government said it was fighting to stop the spread of communism, but opponents of the war believed it was an attempt to take control of Southeast Asia. Millions of young people were drafted into the military, and millions more protested against the Vietnam War. Parents and children often stood on opposite sides of the debate over the war. This debate caused many arguments and much unhappiness in the home, but it was not the only serious problem facing parents. As their children grew up and began to leave, many parents found themselves unhappy.

The American middle class had achieved success and prosperity by now, and they wanted to enjoy it. The working class, too, was generally well-off in the mid-1960s, with good jobs available in manufacturing. For the poorest families, government social programs offered a "safety net" to help them get by financially. Even for a family on welfare, there was hope that life would get better.

Such hope was based on the belief that hard work would bring success. This positive attitude was important to every American social group. In few other countries could people succeed no matter what their family background happened to be. Most Americans believed opportunity was waiting for those who were willing to work for it.

After almost two decades of growth, Americans had good reason to expect happiness. Yet many were not satisfied with their way of life. Although they were far better off than past generations had been, millions of Americans wanted to do more than acquire material things. They needed deeper meaning to their lives.

Cars, Golden Arches, and Electric Knives

The automobile, more than any other feature of American culture, was the symbol of the nation. Families were more mobile than ever. The United States was the most motorized country in the world. In 1968, there were 100 million licensed drivers and 98 million vehicles using 4 million miles of roads.

In the suburbs and in the country, there was little public transportation such as trains or buses. Cars were absolutely essential. Almost everything a family did required an automobile: commuting, shopping, driving kids here and there, visiting family and friends, dating, and going to movies and restaurants. Businesses were created to profit from America's automobile culture, and they succeeded. In 1960, for example, there were only 100 McDonald's drive-in restaurants. In 1967, there were almost 1,000, and in 1974 there were 3,000. By the end of the 1970s, the golden arches symbol of McDonald's seemed to be everywhere.

Previous American generations had taken day trips by train or bus, but now most tourism depended on the car. More and more families traveled to the new state and national parks for recreation. In 1950, visitors to the park systems had numbered only 33 million. In 1965, more than 121 million Americans visited national parks, almost all by car.

People who wanted to spend long periods on the road began to remodel delivery vans. They added bunks, cabinets, and extra seats for camping and cross-country trips. By the 1970s, remodeled vans were so popular that automobile companies were build-

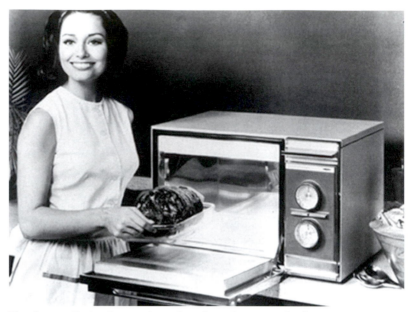

The Amana Radar Range, introduced in 1967, was the first microwave oven. (Coutesy of Amana, Inc.)

ing them new. Next they built "campers," which were larger than vans and had all the conveniences of home.

One sign of a family's success was the electric carving knife, introduced in 1963 in time for Father's Day. The electric knife was considered a "man's gift," perfect for slicing turkey or roasts at family occasions.

More household gadgets were invented each year. They all promised to free the mother from the labor of housework and cooking. In the 1970s, the first home food processor, known as a Cusinart, made cutting and chopping food seem effortless. The microwave oven also appeared during this time and was extremely popular. By 1975, microwave ovens outsold gas ranges. To make daily life even more convenient, all sorts of processed food, ready to heat and eat, filled the shelves of supermarkets across the country.

No Time for Mom

Despite all the time-saving appliances and prepackaged food, the homemaker's labors were far from ended. Whatever hours the mother of the family saved in food preparation were easily spent in other ways. For instance, her children were involved in highly organized activities such as team sports, clubs, and social groups. It was the mother who usually brought them there and picked them up again. Since her husband often came home late from work, dinner time was no longer a family hour together. Anyway, the children might be off at an activity at the dinner hour. So the traditional sit-down family dinner became less important, even impossible. Still, the mother had to see they all were fed, even if it was at different times.

In time, it turned out that the mother was not around as much either. Many women were returning to the workplace. They took jobs that brought in extra money to make ends meet or to help pay for their children's college. In 1960, working mothers with children under the age of seventeen numbered 58 million, compared to 40 million working mothers in 1950.

Although employment made its own demands on her time and energy, the working mother struggled to do her best for the children. Then, suddenly, they were grown and going away to college or the military. Parents who had been devoted to their families found themselves alone. A new challenge faced them: did they want to stay together?

Divorce in the "Age of Anxiety"

The 1950s had been called the "golden years of the family," because family life had seemed stable and secure. That decade had the lowest divorce rates of the past fifty years. Yet many couples had felt trapped in unhappy lives during those years. They had stayed together for the sake of the children, but in the mid-1960s, thousands finally began to divorce. New laws made it far easier to divorce. In the past, one partner had to present a reason, or grounds, for breaking up. This meant proving it was the other person's fault that they had to divorce. By the early 1970s, most states granted divorce by mutual consent of the partners. These were termed *no-fault divorces.*

In 1965, 479,000 couples divorced. Just ten years later, in 1975, that figure more than doubled, as 1.03 million marriages broke up. Between the mid-1950s and mid-1960s, the divorce rate was 2.3 divorces per 1,000 population. This rate rose until it reached a peak of 5.4 per thousand by 1979, with almost 1.2 million divorces that year.

Divorces were often the result of failed expectations. For example, the suburban lifestyle had turned out less ideal than the couple had anticipated when newlyweds. The single-family home in the suburbs often brought about a feeling of isolation from the rest of the world. This isolation was increased by so many Americans traveling to work in cars, alone, instead of using public transportation. Also, instead of going out in public for entertainment, most people stayed home to watch television. An evening in front of the television was the favorite past-time for almost half the population.

Another cause of loneliness was that many families had moved away from their hometowns. They no longer had parents, grandparents, aunts, uncles, and cousins to give support and companionship.

Even the modern comforts of air conditioning isolated people. Air conditioning kept people indoors on steamy summer evenings. Past generations would have been chatting on front stoops, meeting on apartment-house rooftops, or strolling outside. The result was that many Americans had no sense of close community. Even in a busy mall or in a downtown neighborhood, they felt like strangers who were not in touch with those around them. One sociologist called this feeling of isolation the "lonely crowd."

Since World War II, ambitious parents had been one-pointed in their rush for success. By the 1960s, many were tired of the daily "rat race" and sick of competing with others who were as ambitious as themselves. They wanted a fresh start in their lives. Although most couples were able to work out their difficulties and remain together, others saw no choice but to divorce. Most of those who did divorce were not set against marriage, for they soon remarried.

Divorce and remarriage meant the family was no longer defined as a single unit of two parents and their children. The family became "extended" as never before. It included stepparents, stepbrothers and stepsisters, half brothers and sisters, and all their aunts and uncles.

Children whose parents were still together often lived with the anxiety that their own families would dissolve. Some have called the second half of the twentieth century "The Age of Anxiety," and with good reason. The long struggle of so many American parents to create the perfect home often failed to create happiness. At the same time, the family itself was changing. No one knew how it would turn out. Over all this hung the threat of total destruction in a nuclear war.

Fallout Shelters and the Affluent Society

The possibility of nuclear war was a powerful influence on the family and society. This threat especially affected young children. Air-raid drills at school and thoughts of enemy missiles aimed at their hometowns made children fear their world might be blown up at any moment.

In the early 1960s, most Americans thought full-scale war probably would break out with the communist countries. How could the family protect itself from a missile attack? The government's answer was to suggest that families build bomb shelters in the backyard. Thousands of people did just that. These small, underground chambers were made of concrete and stocked with food and water. Televisions and radios were placed inside to listen for the news of the "all-clear" so the family could come out again. Some shelters had exercise equipment to keep the family healthy during a lengthy crisis.

The government was serious about shelters, but most baby boomers made fun of them. They knew that no one could survive a direct nuclear attack. A nuclear strike would contaminate the country with radioactivity and life would be impossible, even far from the explosions.

Many in the younger generation were angry with their parents for putting the world in such a dangerous position. Their fear of nuclear destruction sometimes fueled a philosophy of "live for today."

In these years, the United States was called the "affluent society" because it had so much more than any other nation. Advertising and the government urged Americans to consume as much as they could to keep the economy growing. Consumers were persuaded to buy the latest products, use more of the country's natural resources, and never be satisfied with what they had.

Millions of young people did not agree with this "mindless consumption." They sought change, for the sake of peace and for the future health of the nation they would soon inherit.

Fallout shelter signs, typically colored bright yellow, were a common sight in the 1960s. (Library of Congress)

High Ideals, Hippies, and Hot Tempers

Parents had done their best to give their children everything. At the same time, most also taught their children to honor America's highest ideals. Among those ideals was that all people were entitled to equal rights. And another was that the nation was dedicated to world peace.

In the 1960s, many young Americans wanted these ideals put into practice. They asked why there had to be nuclear confrontation. Why did people live in fear? Why were they at war in Vietnam? Why did parents work so hard all the time to buy the latest cars, the fanciest household appliances, the newest televisions?

Not every American social group thought such questions were the most important ones. African Americans, whether middle-class or living in poverty, had other questions. These had to do with social justice. Why were they discriminated against? Why did blacks lack equal opportunities for education and for jobs?

During the 1960s, thousands of young people took to the streets to protest American involvement in the Vietnam War. Many adults saw the protests as a breakdown in traditional values. (Library of Congress)

When would the United States honor its Constitution, which declared everyone equal under the law? Why should so many poor black men have to serve as soldiers in Vietnam when middle-class white men were allowed to go to college instead?

These and similar questions were at the heart of American family life in the 1960s. At the same time, plenty of Americans were happy to conform to society's standards and did not ask such questions. They saw no need for social change, no problem with consumerism or with the rat race. As a result, people took sides on the day's important social issues. One side was strongly in favor of social justice and demanded change. The other side believed Americans should not complain so much but just be grateful to be living in the United States.

A large part of the younger generation enjoyed an easy lifestyle compared to the youth of the past. While in college, for example, young people were free from the need to work at a job for a living. Their parents and grandparents often thought young people had it too easy.

By the end of the 1960s, deep hostility had developed between two main sections of society, which were generally known as the "Establishment" and "The Movement." The Establishment mostly included conservatives, the older generation, and the government. The Movement included liberals, civil-rights activists, and people of all ages who wanted social justice and peace. The Movement was sometimes termed a *countercul-ture*, meaning its ideas went against the ideas of the country's main culture. The media called some of The Movement's members *hippies*. This term came from "hip," a word describing those who considered themselves more aware, more alert, than the rest of society.

Controversy fired up the United States in the 1960s and early 1970s, sometimes turning violent in the streets. This same controversy also raged in the home. Families often had bitter arguments over the Vietnam War or the younger generation's behavior. Harsh words were exchanged. As they argued, their living-room televisions showed the day's latest news: civil-rights protests, the Berlin Wall with its armed guards, bloody battles in the jungles of Vietnam.

The family conflict that resulted from this clash of cultures was not to be found in old television shows like *Leave it to*

Beaver or *The Adventures of Ozzie and Harriet*. Ideal families on the screen were not of interest to the new generation. The satire of shows such as *Laugh-in* and *The Smothers Brothers* appealed to those who wanted America to change its ways. A later program, *All in the Family*, showed how the different generations in one family disagreed about things, but did it with humor that everyone could laugh at.

Like so many of their parents, young people were searching for meaning to their lives. Among other things, they called for a society that did not limit personal freedoms. They wanted the government to legalize drugs such as marijuana. They also believed society should not object to sexual relations outside of marriage. They were not even sure that marriage was necessary anymore. Young people who were part of The Movement often met together, seated on the floor, in "rap sessions"—discussion groups. They listened to folk and rock music with lyrics that spoke about their own lives. Often they smoked marijuana, though it was illegal and they could go to jail if caught.

Some tried going "back to the land" to live close to nature, far from the pressures of conformity and consumption. They grew their own food and sewed their own clothes. They studied traditional medicine and religions different from those they had known as children.

Troubled parents found themselves trying to communicate with a bearded son whose "hippie-style" hair was shoulder-length. Their daughter might have a colorful bandanna over her own long, straight hair and wear jeans or an old-fashioned, ankle-length "granny dress." Her mother, of course, wished she would wear the neat, pleated skirt and sweater that the older generation had favored. Most parents were angrily against marijuana and any other drugs that were supposed to alter the mind or change the user's senses. Then the parents continued to drink alcohol and smoke tobacco, although the Surgeon General had warned in 1964 that cigarettes could shorten their lives. Their children said this was a "double standard," meaning certain powerful drugs were socially acceptable while other drugs were not. These double standards of parents were considered dishonest by their offspring.

By the end of the 1970s, much of this family conflict had calmed down, as members came to accept each other and their different beliefs.

"Family," Women, and Happy Marriage

In the 1960s and 1970s, divorce broke up 15 million American families, but many more were formed, often by remarriage. The family began to take on a different shape.

The idea of "family" continued to be important, but its definition changed. A family was no longer defined only as a living group with a father who was the breadwinner, a wife who was the homemaker, and their children. Now the family could be a divorced mother or father with children. It could be a remarried couple, each with his or her own children. Also, there were large numbers of unwed parents who had no plans to marry.

Growing numbers of single mothers were raising children, usually with the help of parents or grandparents. The fathers of these children sometimes had abandoned them or had moved out of the house due to divorce, or simply refused to live with them. In the 1960s, approximately 4.5 million households were headed by single women. That number grew to 8.7 million by 1980.

By the end of the 1970s, American women had more independence than ever. The development of birth control methods in the 1960s and the legalization of abortion in 1973 gave a woman reproductive freedom. She could have no babies, or as many as she chose. At this time, women of child-bearing age averaged fewer than two children each. In the 1950s, the average number of children for each woman of child-bearing age had been 3.7.

This poster promoting the birth-control pill used Uncle Sam to spread its message.
(Library of Congress)

Between 1960 and the late 1970s, the nation's birthrate declined from 23.7 per 1,000 population to 14.9. This was due, in part, to the fact that many couples were choosing not to have children at all. Also, an increasing number of people preferred to live alone. In 1980, 18.3 million persons lived on their own, compared with approximately 7 million in 1960.

Happily married couples of the 1970s often wanted more from their marriage than child rearing, homemaking, and breadwinning. Many modern parents wanted to fully enjoy their married life. They wanted to travel, go out to dinner and shows, and get the most out of life as a loving couple. Having fewer children gave them more time for themselves.

Also, modern couples waited longer after marriage to have children. This gave a woman a chance to build her own career before she became a mother. Often new mothers returned to their careers as soon as possible, and the child was cared for by others. The rise of community day-care centers filled a growing need for watching over little children whose parents were at work. In 1974, almost 4.7 million children were in day care—an increase of 21 percent over 1967.

In these years, the federal government established Project Head Start to care for the children of needy families during the day. One of this program's most important tasks was to help very young children prepare for school. The parents of these children were also involved in Head Start, learning how to make better homes.

A Struggling Economy and Home Entertainment

As the 1970s closed, memories of the Vietnam War slowly withdrew, and Americans looked forward to a time of peace. The country's prosperity, however, also seemed a thing of the past.

Serious economic downturns caused businesses to fail, and many people lost their jobs. To make things worse, U.S. industry moved more and more factories overseas, where salaries were much lower. As a result, the working class lost well-paying man-ufacturing jobs that had made it comfortable since World War II.

In spite of the country's economic troubles, there was plenty of new entertainment in the American home. Television pro-gramming expanded as many new cable broadcasts became available. Televised sports grew in popularity. In the 1970s, Atari added to the electronic entertainment mix by producing the first low-priced television games. The video cassette recorder, or VCR, became popular, allowing viewers to tape programs for later viewing. Most families had more than one television.

The average family was now addicted to television. Not only did parents watch entertainment and news programs, their chil-dren played electronic games almost nonstop. Americans were being prepared for the approaching computer revolution of the 1980s. When the personal computer suddenly burst into the American family's daily life, it was transformed forever.

Chapter Two

Social and Political Attitudes

The 1960s and 1970s were periods of social turmoil and national growth. These decades were marked by the unpopular Vietnam War, continuing tension with the Soviet Union, the assassinations of several national leaders, and the fight for equal rights for African Americans and other minorities as well as for women.

During the 1960s, many gains were made in the area of civil rights. The federal government also made ending poverty in America a major goal. By 1973, the nation had ended its involvement in the Vietnam War.

Although many Americans saw these developments as positive, each of these struggles had divided the nation. To make matters worse, Americans learned that one of their presidents, Richard Nixon, had abused his power by ordering a burglary on the office of his opponents and then lied to cover it up. In 1974, he was forced to resign.

When the presidents that followed him struggled with a weak economy, and finally the taking of fifty-three Americans as hostages by Islamic fundamentalists in the Middle East nation of Iran, many Americans began looking for new leadership.

Members of the American Legion (LEFT) **prepare for Fourth of July celebrations** (National Archives)**; young protesters at an antiwar rally in 1968** (RIGHT)**.** (Library of Congress)

Cold War Crises

A period of competition between the United States and the Soviet Union known as the Cold War began immediately after World War II ended in 1945. By 1960, the Cold War had entered a crisis stage as John F. Kennedy's presidency began. When the Soviet Union placed missiles in Cuba—ninety miles off the coast of Florida—Kennedy threatened attack if they were not removed. His orders to start blockade, or block all ships or planes coming into or going from Cuba, brought about a thirteen-day standoff with the Soviets. The danger of war ended when Soviet premier Nikita Khrushchev finally agreed to withdraw the missiles. Another major crisis occurred when communist East Germany built a wall through the capital city of Berlin to keep East Germans from escaping to the West. For the next three decades, the Berlin Wall was perhaps the most famous symbol of the hostility between the free world and the communist bloc.

The Civil Rights Movement

There were tensions at home in America, too. African Americans were winning civil rights in federal court cases, but local and state governments in the South were slow to put them into effect. At the same time, blacks were among the poorest Americans. Many had little hope of better living conditions. President Kennedy set out to create legislation that would improve housing and educational and employment opportunities.

Kennedy had little success in Congress. Conservatives there opposed poverty programs and new government laws promoting equal rights for minorities. Although some opposed these programs out of racism against African Americans, many others did so because they were against the federal government imposing too many programs and laws on the states.

At the same time, some African Americans grew restless under the philosophy of nonviolent resistance that had guided the movement since the mid-1950s. Some were so angry that they called for taking power into their own hands if necessary. Up until this time, most protests were carried out as "sit-ins" and marches. Blacks and white supporters in hundreds of communities across the nation went where they were not allowed by segregation laws. They "sat in" at "whites-only" lunch counters, in waiting areas of bus and train stations, outside businesses that

A Glamorous Presidency Cut Short

When John F. Kennedy became president in 1960 at the age of forty-three, he became the youngest man ever elected president. (Theodore Roosevelt became the youngest president in history after President William McKinley was assassinated in 1900, but he was not elected on his own until 1904.) Kennedy's youth, good looks, and charm were matched by the same qualities in his wife Jacqueline. Together the couple and their two young children, Caroline and John, Jr., became favorites with the press and the American public. His popularity would remain high throughout his presidency.

Sadly, Kennedy's term in office was a short one. On November 22, 1963, President Kennedy visited Dallas, Texas, where many people bitterly opposed some of his policies. Kennedy was in Texas to meet with the state's Democratic leaders, and he joined them in a motorcade—a parade of automobiles—through Dallas. As he and Jacqueline sat waving from an open limousine, rifle shots rang out, and the president was struck twice. He was hurried away but died before he reached the hospital.

Dallas resident Lee Harvey Oswald was immediately arrested and accused of the assassination. Within two days, Oswald was murdered in the Dallas police station, shot by a local man in revenge for the killing of Kennedy.

John F. Kennedy giving his inaugural address. (Library of Congress)

discriminated against blacks, and in schools. They were often attacked and beaten by mobs and then jailed by local police for causing the violence.

Still, most did not resist violently. Television newscasters showed the demonstrators being attacked by police and civilians. All across the nation, millions of whites came to realize how wrong segregation was and how courageous the demonstrators were. Still, opposition from some state and local governments was strong. In 1962, Alabama governor George C. Wallace

Malcolm X

Malcolm X (Library of Congress)

Born in Omaha, Nebraska in 1925, Malcolm Little changed his name and his life when he learned about the Nation of Islam while in prison for burglary. Nation of Islam leader Elijah Muhammad argued that African Americans should not try to integrate with whites. He said it was better for African Americans to stay separate.

Taking the name Malcolm X to remind people that the name "Little" had been forced on his enslaved ancestors by white masters, Malcolm became a minister for the Nation of Islam in New York City's Harlem. Unlike Dr. Martin Luther King, Jr., he argued that African Americans had the right to defend themselves "by any means necessary," including the use of violence.

As Malcolm's influence grew, Elijah Muhammad became jealous. In December 1963, Malcolm left the organization. He travelled to Mecca, a holy place for Muslims, in Saudi Arabia. There he met Muslims who preached equality of the races. It changed his outlook, and when he returned home, he again changed his name to El-Hajj Malik El-Shabazz (*el-haj mal-EEK el-shuh-BAZ*). He still believed that racism was to blame for the lack of equality in the United States, but he stopped hating whites. He began urging blacks to identify with people of African heritage from around the world. He preached unity and stressed the need for African Americans to take control of their own futures.

Malcom believed that members of the Nation of Islam wanted him dead because he rejected the separation of black and white societies. On February 21, 1965, Malcolm X was addressing a crowd in Harlem. Three men shot him and he died instantly at age thirty-nine. His death revealed the deep divisions in the African American Muslim community.

African American adults and children march for civil rights in Selma, Alabama. (Library of Congress)

blocked the door of the University of Alabama, trying to prevent the first black students from entering. Wallace failed, and the efforts at winning civil rights continued.

Black and white "Freedom Riders" traveled by bus across the South to challenge segregated bus stations. They, too, were often attacked by mobs while police watched. In time, the federal government was forced to step in and prevent violence. The government often sent federal marshals or troops to keep the peace. However, no one could stop all the cruelty. In 1963, the bombing of a Birmingham, Alabama, church killed four African American girls. (No arrests would be made until 1977, when the first of four suspects in the bombing was convicted and jailed. Two others would finally be convicted in 2002 of participating in the bombing. The fourth suspect died before facing charges. All four had been members of the racist hate group the Ku Klux Klan.) The bombing came soon after a massive civil rights march on Washington, D.C., by more than 250,000 Americans. The protesters called for the federal government to do more for civil rights.

Although Kennedy had not been able to get effective civil-rights legislation through Congress, his successor did. Lyndon B. Johnson, Kennedy's vice president, had been one of the most powerful members of Congress. When he assumed the presidency,

Johnson pushed for the laws Kennedy had wanted. A Texan who had been raised in difficult rural conditions, Johnson understood the situation many blacks faced. He got Congress to pass the 1964 Civil Rights Act prohibiting racial and gender discrimination. The next year, Johnson pushed for the Voting Rights Act. This law prohibited barriers that prevented African Americans from voting.

Advances in civil rights did not prevent summer race riots in the inner cities. In the mid-1960s, some frustrated African Americans began to take to the streets, and riots broke out. The worst riot was in 1965, when the Watts section of Los Angeles became a battle zone. Stores were looted, cars and buildings burned, and rioters fought with police and national guard troops. After six days of rioting, which required 14,000 guardsman to control, thirty persons were dead and 900 injured.

Frustration among African Americans also led to a split in the Civil Rights movement. Some younger African American leaders, such as Stokely Carmichael and Malcolm X began calling for African Americans to defend themselves with violence if necessary when attacked.

LBJ and the Great Society

After becoming president, Lyndon Johnson enjoyed widespread public support among the population. Johnson knew well that the Democratic Party would lose its base in the South because of his civil rights policies. Still, he went ahead with them. The political opposition to civil rights legislation reorganized. Southern Democrats supported Barry Goldwater, the 1964 Republican presidential candidate. The conservative Goldwater had voted against the Civil Rights Act because he believed it gave the federal government too much power and took rights away from the states. In the election, Johnson and the Democrats won a landslide victory despite losing the powerful southern wing of the party.

While promoting civil rights legislation, Johnson also declared a nationwide campaign known as the War on Poverty. In 1964, Congress passed the Equal Opportunity Act, aimed at helping the poor. The act established job-training programs and organized volunteers to work with the poor in their own neighborhoods. It made loans available to low-income farmers and small businesses that would not normally qualify. The Head Start program was established to help preschool children from poor homes prepare for school.

Other programs sprang from Johnson's War on Poverty to improve education and job opportunities. Some were designed to help young people get out of their rundown neighborhoods and attend college. Others helped teach the poor to take charge of their own lives. These included registering to vote and organizing local alliances such as tenant unions, to stand up for their rights. These Community Action Programs helped many inner-city people make their votes count when choosing political leaders. Antipoverty programs also extended into remote areas of Appalachia, where poor whites had been isolated for generations.

The War on Poverty had great success in many ways. The number of families living below the poverty line declined dramatically over these decades.

Johnson's far-reaching policies brought about reforms in civil rights and society. Together they were known as the Great Society policy. They included legislation for the improvement of housing, transportation, urban development, public education, health care, and aid to the elderly. In 1965, the Medicare program was established by Congress to provide health insurance for the elderly. This was followed by Medicaid, which helped pay for medical care to the needy.

Vietnam War and the Antiwar Movement

As the federal government worked to improve lives at home, it continued to work against the spread of communism overseas. In addition to facing the Cuban Missile and Berlin Wall crises, President Kennedy also began the United States' involvement in a war between the southeast Asian country of communist North Vietnam and anticommunist South Vietnam. Beginning with several hundred unofficial advisors arriving in Vietnam in 1963, and reaching as many as more than half a million soldiers by the late 1960s, the Vietnam War divided the nation like no other war had up to that time. Many believed that the war was a just cause in the battle against communist aggression. Many others came to believe that the war was not just and that the United States was using its power on a small regional civil war to undo the will of that nation's people.

As President Johnson called for an increase in the military

draft (or mandatory service), many young Americans were among the first to oppose the war. Many of those activists, as they were called, were college students who were exempt, or exused, from service as long as they remained in school.

Many activists wanted their colleges and universities to question America's involvement in the war in Vietnam. Across the nation, students and instructors held teach-ins to discuss arguments for and against the war. Many activists did not think this was enough. They demanded that their colleges and universities oppose the conflict. They wanted to close down officer-training courses and forbid laboratory research into military technology on campus. Activists also wanted administrators and trustees to challenge the government's reasons for waging the war. Much antiwar opposition developed on campuses, but few educational institutions took formal stands against the Vietnam War.

Other Campus Issues

Many college students during the 1960s were also active in the Civil Rights movement. Large numbers of students opposed the social system that kept minorities down and forced the middle class to conform to strict traditions. These students organized themselves into campus associations to demonstrate for student rights and for change.

Students wanted their colleges to set examples on social issues of the day. For example, many students called for more minorities to be admitted and for new "minority studies" courses that explored racial and social injustice. Professors and students were encouraged to openly discuss how to achieve world peace and remove the constant threat of nuclear war.

When students took part in campus riots in 1964–1965, many older Americans considered them to be spoiled and ungrateful. A division emerged between the pro-war and antiwar groups.

Nixon Comes to Power

All the while, the Vietnam War raged. Television satellite news, broadcast from the front lines, brought the horrors of war into American living rooms. By 1968, antiwar sentiment was much more widespread. The question of what was true patriotism was debated in homes, in houses of worship, in Congress, and on the streets.

In the midst of these debates, a tragedy occurred. In April of that year, Dr. Martin Luther King, Jr., who had spent the previous twenty years preaching nonviolence as a way to bring equality to African Americans, was shot and killed by a lone gunman.

As the United States headed into the 1968 presidential election, the country was more deeply divided than ever. Many people felt that the country was facing a complete breakdown of law and order. Some of those people demanded the protesters stop their civil disobedience. At the same time, those who wanted change in government policies and society continued to demand that America put civil rights laws into effect and also stop the war.

By the spring of 1968, President Johnson's popularity was at an all-time low. Even so, the country was stunned when he announced that he would not seek reelection that year. He decided to resign after major enemy counterattacks showed that American military policy in Vietnam had been a failure. Assessments of the war's progress had been filled with inaccurate statements. One leading general declared the end of the war to be at hand. He said we could "see the light at the end of the tunnel." This became one of the most memorable statements about the futility of the Vietnam War. The end of the tunnel was not in sight. Until the bloody fighting that opened 1968, Americans had thought they were winning the war.

With Johnson's announcement that he would not run for president, his vice president, Hubert Humphrey of Minnesota, joined the antiwar candidates Senators Eugene McCarthy, also of Minnesota, and Robert F. Kennedy of New York for the Democratic nomination. In June, Kennedy, a brother of the late president, won the California primary to become the favorite to win the nomination. Shortly after his victory speech, however, he too was assassinated.

In the end, Humphrey won the Democratic nomination only to lose the 1968 election to Republican Richard M. Nixon. Nixon, from California, had been vice president under Eisenhower. The Nixon campaign was aided by the campaign of Southerner George Wallace, whose American Independent Party drew off Democratic votes.

During his presidency, Nixon called for the support of Americans who did not march in the streets or speak out publicly but agreed with him. He called them the "silent majority."

A "Nixon for President" campaign button.
(private collection)

Nixon claimed he had a secret plan to end the war in Vietnam and to end the military draft. It required seven more years and immense political pressure before either was achieved. Republicans won control of the once-Democratic "Solid South" by calling for stronger states' rights and a return to law and order.

Women Organize

Although at first not as visible as the "antiwar" or civil rights movements, the effort for women's rights was gaining strength. President Kennedy had established the Presidential Commission on Women in 1961 to study the woman's place in society. The commission proved that women were discriminated against, just like minorities. All the states eventually established similar commissions for examining the status of women. The first federal legislation to guarantee women's rights was the Equal Pay Act of 1963.

One of the great influences upon women of this time was Betty Friedan's *The Feminine Mystique*. This 1963 book openly discussed the dissatisfaction of many middle-class women with their lives and place in society. For the first time, many women realized that others shared similar experiences. They began to take charge of their lives and create new plans for the future.

A groundswell of discussion and debate caused millions of women to rethink their lives. The modern women's liberation movement came into existence at this time. The National Organization for Women (NOW) was established in 1966 as one of the first modern associations working for equal rights. That same year, the term *Ms.* appeared as a way to address women. Ms. did not take into account their status as married (Mrs.) or unmarried (Miss).

A year before, the women's magazine *Ms.* was founded, and it was an immediate success. The magazine dealt with topics beyond traditional matters of home and garden, child-rearing, and beauty. Politics, sexuality, and women's liberation were key *Ms.* themes. Near the close of the decade, *Ms.* sold more than 850,000 copies a month.

In 1973, those who favored a women's right to choose whether or not to abort, or end a pregnancy, won a controversial victory when the U.S. Supreme Court ruled that women do have the right to end their pregnancies during the first trimester, or

Betty Friedan's book *The Feminine Mystique* helped start the feminist movement. In 1966, Friedan cofounded the National Organization for Women. (Library of Congress)

three months of becoming pregnant. Many women argued that this decision gave them the right to control their own bodies. Others argued that abortion was morally wrong and that under no circumstances should ending a pregnancy be allowed. This debate continues to the present.

One effort of the women's movement did not fully succeed, however. This was the Equal Rights Amendment to the Constitution. This proposed amendment forbade discrimination on account of gender. Passage required thirty-eight state legislatures to vote for its approval, but only thirty-five did so. The proposed amendment ran out of time for ratification and died early in the 1980s.

War and Watergate

The Vietnam War seemed to be cooling down by 1970, but then came news of secret American attacks in Cambodia. President Nixon had led the public to believe that the war would be ending soon, so the news that it had actually widened to another country came as a surprise. Protests against widening the war started all over again, with deadly results.

In this year, Ohio national guardsmen opened fire on demonstrating students at Kent State University, killing and wounding several. Some casualties were bystanders just looking on. Soon afterward, an antiwar rally in New York City was violently attacked by hundreds of pro-war construction workers.

Nixon won the 1972 election by a landslide, defeating Democrat George McGovern of South Dakota. This same year, Nixon made the surprise decision to visit Communist China. This was against his longtime anticommunist stance. Nixon's visit opened the door to China for the first time since 1949.

Another event of 1972 was fatal to Nixon's presidency. Agents of his Republican election committee were discovered burglarizing the Democratic committee's national headquarters. This became known as the Watergate scandal, after the building that held the Democratic headquarters. The president's top aides were convicted of crimes related to the break-in and cover-up. Nixon refused to turn over secret tape recordings to investigators. After almost two years of hearings and investigation, Congress prepared to impeach the president.

Nixon admitted he had kept the FBI from investigating White House involvement in the Watergate scandal. He soon resigned in disgrace, the first president ever to do so. Vice President Gerald Ford of Michigan became president and immediately pardoned Nixon. This meant the former president could not be tried for any crimes he had committed while president.

A year later, Ford was president when the Vietnam War finally came to an end, and American troops were brought home.

The Carter Presidency

A "Jimmy Carter for President" campaign button.
(private collection)

Gerald Ford lost the 1976 presidential election to Jimmy Carter, former governor of Georgia. Carter made his run for president without the support of major contributors, such as big businesses. This meant he was unusually independent as president.

Almost immediately, the new president pardoned men who had left the country to avoid serving in the Vietnam War. This earned Carter the disapproval of some and the admiration of others.

Carter established policies that pressured foreign nations to improve the treatment of their citizens. Carter did not want to cooperate or trade with nations that had governments that did not recognize their peoples' human rights. He also held the United States to honor its treaty with Panama, returning the strategic Panama Canal to that country in 1979. At the same time, he engineered a crucial peace treaty between Egypt and Israel.

Carter's efforts to achieve reforms in American elections, welfare, energy, and the environment were met with stiff opposition in Congress. He was largely unsuccessful in changing government bureaucracy or its policies. Still, he was highly respected as a humanitarian.

The Iran Hostage Crisis

In 1979, Iranians overthrew their government, which had been led by a shah, or king. The shah fled the country and went to the United States, his ally for many years. That November, Iranian revolutionaries made prisoners of the American embassy staff in Teheran, the capital, and demanded the return of the shah. They intended to put him on trial as a tyrant who had committed crimes against the people. The United States refused to send him back, and a "hostage crisis" developed, lasting 444 days.

After the disaster of Vietnam, the thought of another war repelled many Americans. The lives of the hostages were at risk, but the nation seemed unable to do anything about it. President Carter was harshly attacked for his inability to free the hostages. In 1980, at the height of the crisis, Carter ran for a second term. His Republican opponent was former California governor Ronald Reagan. With the hostages still imprisoned during the campaign, Carter's reputation was badly tarnished. Some people accused the Reagan campaign of making a secret deal with the Iranians, promising to sell them arms if they held the hostages through the campaign, although the charge was never proven.

Carter was soundly defeated, with 36.5 million popular votes to Reagan's 43.9 million. Two days before Ronald Reagan's swearing-in as president, Iran announced it would free the hostages.

Chapter Three

Education

An African American student (LEFT) **in a Black Studies class in Chicago in 1973 reads a book about great rulers in Africa's past. Students raise their hands in a classroom** (RIGHT) **at Leakey, Texas, near San Antonio, also in 1973.** (National Archives)

Educating their children was the most important ambition of the parents of baby boomers, after food and housing. The baby boom generation expected to go to college the way their parents had expected to go to high school. In 1960, more than 43 percent of Americans between the ages of twenty-five and twenty-nine had completed high school. That figure rose to more than 68 percent by 1980.

The number of students kept growing as baby boomers flooded schools during the 1960s and 1970s. The civil-rights movement and decisions by the courts opened doors to education for millions of young people who previously had been shut out. These included African Americans, the poor, and handicapped children. At the same time, new educational opportunity was offered to girls, who for the first time were treated as the equals of boys.

During these decades, women and minorities attended college in steadily increasing numbers. In 1960, approximately 33 percent of the more than 392,000 college graduates were women. The numbers grew, and in 1980, women accounted for 47 percent of the almost 1 million students who graduated that year. In 1970, total college enrollment was 5.7 million, including 422,000 African American students. College enrollment grew to almost 10.2 million by 1980. African Americans counted for more than 1 million of the total.

In the mid-1960s, major changes took place in education. Both presidents from that era, John F. Kennedy and Lyndon B. Johnson, were determined to fight poverty in America. They believed that improving education and literacy (the ability to read and write) were keys to solving poverty. Thanks to the visions of these presidents, reforming and strengthening education became a major goal of the federal government. Over the next fifteen years, billions of dollars from federal and state governments were pumped into public school systems and higher education. More than ever before, in the 1960s and 1970s, American parents and educators united in an effort to improve the schools.

Yet 1980's test scores proved that students were learning less than previous generations had learned. In 1940, almost 97 percent of Americans could read and write. That figure dropped steadily during the 1960s and 1970s. By 1980, approximately 20 percent of the population was illiterate—unable to read or write. The rate of illiteracy would go even higher, reaching 25 percent later in the century.

There was growing controversy over why American children seemed less well-educated than many children in western Europe and Asia. Americans were asking just how good their schools were. A movement to reform curriculum in this period did not improve education. Test scores dropped, and public confidence in teachers weakened. There followed a strong back-to-the-basics movement that emphasized reading, writing, and arithmetic. Teachers and administrators found themselves on the firing line.

By the 1980s, the school-age population began declining. The nation's public schools had gone through eighty years of constant and often painful growth. Now the quality of that growth had to be addressed.

Education and the "Great Society"

Government influence on education increased in the 1960s. In 1963, the Supreme Court ruled that no public school could conduct prayer or religious observances. Federal powers over education grew further when Congress passed the Civil Rights Act of 1964. This act outlawed racial discrimination in schools and other institutions that received federal aid.

The U.S. public-education system was changed forever by the Elementary and Secondary Education Act passed by Congress in

Rising High-School Graduation Rate

The chart below shows the rising percentage of white and African American students who graduated from high school between 1964 and 1980.

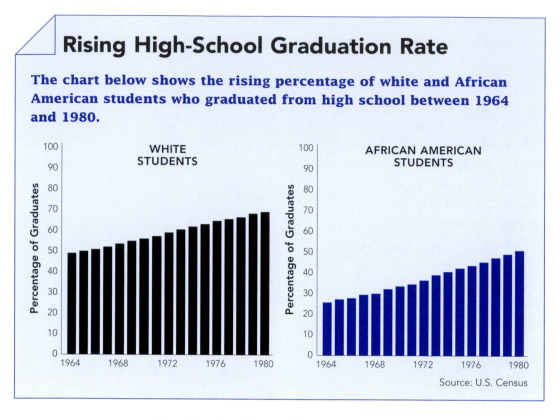

Source: U.S. Census

1965. This legislation offered millions of federal dollars to higher education, state education departments, and local school districts. Known as the Education Act, it also created programs to help schools that had large numbers of poor children. President Johnson used all his political influence to get the Education Act through Congress. "I will never do anything in my entire life, now or in the future, that excites me more, or benefits the nation I serve more . . . than what we have done with this education bill," he said.

Also in 1965, Congress passed legislation that provided funds for college libraries, classroom equipment, research, and teacher-training programs. In addition, it established federally backed student loan programs for college and vocational education.

In the following years, Congress passed more acts to further aid students who had special needs. These included the Bilingual Education Act, the Native American Education Act, and the Education for All Handicapped Children Act. Most of the programs created by this new legislation helped people who were suffering from poverty or discrimination. As a result, these programs increased the number of students attending high school.

In 1969, 77 percent of seventeen-year-olds had a high school diploma. This was the highest percent in history. That number fell from then on, dropping to less than 70 percent in the 1990s.

Education and Integration

Billions of federal dollars were offered to higher education, state education departments, and local school districts. To get that money, schools had to accept government standards in education. This was a major change for most state and local administrators.

Until this time, schools had been controlled locally. They were mainly paid for by state and local taxes. Now the national government was gaining influence over education because it gave funds to those schools that met new standards. For example, to receive government funding, schools had to be racially integrated. If a school district or college did not integrate, it would lose millions in federal money. Local educators who wanted federal funds were forced to change their racial policies.

When federal courts required an end to racial segregation in the 1950s, most Southern communities at first refused to integrate. Change was slow to come. Integration in education really did not take hold until the mid-1960s. The offer of federal education funds did much to encourage that change.

Johnson's Great Society policies included making sure minorities were not discriminated against in employment or educational opportunities. In 1967, his administration resolved to "take affirmative (positive) action" to ensure that federal employees were treated "without regard to their race, creed, color, or national origin." Johnson also called for the government to take affirmative action that benefited women.

Generally, affirmative action meant helping those who had been discriminated against. In higher education, affirmative action meant enrolling minority students, even if their academic qualifications were not as high as white students.

Campuses Become Battlegrounds

During the 1960s, some Southern schools and universities endured anti-integration demonstrations and riots. These uprisings had to be stopped by thousands of state and federal troops. Even if the institution had agreed to integrate, many whites angrily opposed it.

In 1962, James H. Meredith of Mississippi enrolled as the

first African American at the University of Mississippi. It required a court order to force the all-white university to accept Meredith. When he tried to attend school, hundreds of armed white racists came from around the nation to stop him. President Kennedy sent in thousands of federal troops and marshals to restore order. Pitched battles erupted in the streets, two people were killed, and others wounded. The federal government won, and Meredith was allowed to enroll.

A year later, Governor George C. Wallace stood in the doorway of the University of Alabama to prevent integration. Federal authorities again had to clear the way, although with far less violence. Combined with civil rights protests and demonstrations across the country, the integration of schools in the 1960s changed American society forever.

To make the situation even more tense, debate over the Vietnam War was tearing the nation apart. Discussions about the war were held in high schools and colleges. Powerful antiwar movements developed on many campuses. College students took over administration offices to protest the war. Others rioted, throwing rocks and fighting with police. Demonstrations turned even more violent as the war dragged on.

In 1968, three students were killed at Orangeburg State University in South Carolina when members of the highway patrol fired on demonstrators protesting a segregated bowling alley. Another twenty-seven were wounded. In 1970, National Guardsmen opened fire on a student antiwar protest at Kent State University in Ohio. Four students were killed, and several others wounded. Ten days later, two more students were killed and twelve injured when police and guardsmen fired on a campus demonstration at Jackson State College in Mississippi.

With the winding down of the war by the mid-1970s, student unrest also came to an end. Yet young people were troubled when they finished their studies, because the economy was weak. Jobs were not waiting for college graduates, as they had been during the prosperous war years. And there were more college students than ever before.

At the same time, tuition costs rose dramatically. Many young people could not afford to attend private colleges. As a result, the public state-university systems and two-year colleges grew vigorously.

Busing for Racial Balance in Schools

In order to achieve a more balanced racial mix, public school districts began to bus children to schools in other neighborhoods. If a school had a high percentage of white students, then black students would be brought in from other schools. At the same time, white students were bused to schools with a majority of black students. Changing the racial balance in Northern schools did not go as smoothly as it did in the South.

Southern children had traditionally been divided according to race, even if they lived in the same neighborhoods. In the North, however, many schools were all-black or all-white because that was the makeup of the neighborhood. Local taxes paid much of a school's budget. The poorer black neighborhoods could not contribute as much tax money as could white neighborhoods. The result was that most black schools in the North were inferior to white schools. The classrooms were not as well maintained, teachers were paid less, textbooks were older, and sports and extra-curricular activities were underfunded.

The goal of mandatory, or forced, busing was to give public schools a more racially balanced student body.
(Library of Congress)

Forced busing caused hostility and conflict in the North. Many white parents did not want their children to go to schools where the majority of students were black. Also, the school could be far from the student's home, requiring long bus trips. Racial unrest exploded in some places.

In 1969, a riot broke out between black and white students in a Syracuse, New York, high school. An all-white fraternity threatened black students being bused to the school. The principal was clubbed when he tried to stop the riot, suffering a fractured skull. The school district, parents, and students tried to solve the conflict, but it was difficult. In the next year, the school was closed ten times because of racial clashes.

Full integration of schools in the North was slower coming than in the South. Battles over busing came to a head in the mid-1970s. Boston suffered one of the longest and most painful busing controversies of all. For years, the residents of all-white Boston neighborhoods opposed busing. The law and the mayor's office were against them, however. Boston's forced busing caused many white parents to demonstrate violently. Fighting sometimes broke out as police tried to keep antibusing protesters under control.

In this time, private schools around the nation began a period of steady growth. This was in part because so many white parents opposed busing in public schools. They sent their children to private schools instead. In many Southern communities, most white students abandoned public schools for new segregated academies that sprang up. These often were run by white churches.

Unrest in the public schools was part of the wider social tumult of this time. Opposition to the ongoing Vietnam War combined with the struggle for civil rights to split American society. People took one side or the other, and too often violence was the result—in and out of schools.

Turbulent Times for Schools

Early in the 1960s, thousands of college students called for more free speech and for new courses of study. Idealistic students wanted to improve society. They began with trying to change

An antiwar rally at the University of California, Berkeley (Library of Congress)

their colleges. Later the attempt to change the status quo spread to younger students and the high schools.

College students were successful in winning new courses and free-speech rights. The demand for change in higher education merged into the Civil Rights movement. Many college students protested in favor of racial integration and for a change in American attitudes to race. By the late 1960s, many from "The Movement," as it was called, were active in antiwar demonstrations. These sometimes turned violent. In time, the turbulence spread to high schools all over the country. The struggle again went to the courts for decisions.

In 1965, two Iowa high-school students were suspended from school for wearing black armbands to class to protest the Vietnam War. The students sued in court, claiming their First Amendment rights of free speech had been violated. Four years later, the U.S. Supreme Court agreed. The nation's highest court ruled that student expression cannot be silenced just because the school disagrees with their point of view.

The troubles of society in the 1960s and early 1970s swamped public schools and educators. Schools were being questioned and educators challenged. At the same time, social stresses complicated the lives of young people. For example, the birthrate for unmarried teenagers climbed year after year. So did drug use among high school seniors. The proportion of students who used illegal drugs rose from 31 percent in 1975 to 37 percent in 1980.

To help find answers to their school's troubles, school administrators, teachers, guidance counselors, and nurses cooperated with members of the local PTA (Parent-Teacher Association). Officially known as the National Congress of Parents and Teachers, the PTA had more than 10 million members in the 1970s. The association was founded to foster a closer relationship between home and school. In 1972, the PTA celebrated its seventy-fifth anniversary. With more than 41,000 local chapters, this organization was a powerful force in public education. Parents and teachers worked together to address the needs of schoolchildren, but times were changing fast. Keeping up with change was not easy.

Schools struggled just to maintain order in these years. Many added social services for counseling students. They also attempted to make education more relevant to real life. New teaching theories were adopted to make classroom work less structured. By the mid-1970s, schools were attempting to be more sensitive to the needs of students. The atmosphere in many schools became more relaxed. Too often, however, this meant less emphasis on core curriculum and high achievement.

The 1970s were a time of severe economic difficulties, with high unemployment across the nation. Schools suffered as government funding for public education was cut sharply. At the same time, public education struck out in new directions. The Native American Education Act, for example, opened opportunities for Indian peoples to take charge of their own educations. As a result, interest in traditional ways and cultures was stimulated for many native students. This new impulse would help bring about a dynamic Indian-rights movement over the following decades.

The rights of girls to equal opportunity in schools also became prominent in the 1970s.

Equal Rights in Sports

A major breakthrough in this time was an act of Congress to make participation in public-school activities more fair to girls and women. Passed in 1972, this regulation was known as Title IX of the Education Amendments Act.

For one thing, Title IX required schools to offer girls' sports programs that were equal to boys' programs. A school's commitment to sports had to be the same for both genders. The result was that millions more girls soon had the opportunity to play scholastic and college sports.

In time, old-fashioned concerns about the "weaker" physical and mental strength of girls also began to change. For example, previous rules for girls' basketball did not allow a student to play more than two quarters in a game. Girls played only a half-court game. Also, girls were checked regularly for signs of "overexertion." That soon changed as girls played full-court and without restrictions on minutes in the game.

Within a few years after Title IX took effect in 1975, female athletes had a strong presence in scholastic athletics. Millions more young women joined school and college teams. When there was no girls' team in a sport, Title IX said girls could play on the boys' team. Girls on boys' teams soon helped get rid of the idea that girls were a "weaker sex." It also encouraged administrators to add new girls' teams.

One school superintendent said, "We were getting so many calls from principals asking if girls could play on boys' teams, I said, 'We've got to do something about the girls' program.'" He added, "If it's good for boys, we thought, then it's good for girls."

Title IX opened a floodgate of sports participation for girls. There were about 4 million interscholastic athletes in 1971. Only 7.4 percent of them were girls. In the 1990s, more than 6.4 million students played interscholastic sports, and more than 40 percent, or 2.6 million, were girls.

Thanks to Title IX, more young women were able to participate in school sports. (Library of Congress)

New Ways of Teaching

Through the 1960s and 1970s, attempts were made to reform the curriculum and methods of teaching.

Some educators and parents thought there was more memorization than real learning in schools. They wanted children to learn how to learn rather than just work at rote, or memorized, learning. From now on, the teacher was not to be a disciplinarian or authority figure. Instead, the teacher was to be a guide, more of a coach. Children were supposed to be able to learn better without the pressure of memorizing spelling words or drilling at math.

In this reform movement, teachers were encouraged to be creative in their teaching methods. They were to experiment. Instead of focusing on a textbook and "stay-in-your-seat" learning, students were expected to take more responsibility for what they learned. Schools experimented with "open-concept" education, which gave students more personal freedom. They were allowed more choices, including when they went to a class. This was termed *flexible scheduling*. Another freedom was the right not to attend class at all.

Nongraded courses were put in place in some schools. As a result, students' achievements in nongraded classes were not measured. Students were supposed to learn because they wanted to learn, not just because they were trying to get a good grade.

In the 1960s and early 1970s, "New Math" came to the schools. The former methods of memorizing tables and problems was replaced by a form of logical thinking. This was supposed to be a better way of learning math theory. New Math was believed to make math more meaningful to the student. It also would make the student better able to think and reason.

Critics soon began to object to these unfamiliar methods of education. New Math, they declared, failed to teach such basic important skills as addition and multiplication. Furthermore, teachers and parents did not understand all the theories behind New Math. Thus, it was difficult to explain the subject to students.

By the early 1970s, many teaching experiments had fallen by the wayside. It became obvious that children were not learning the fundamentals. Achievement test scores showed that students were not as well-educated as previous generations. And those scores were getting worse.

In the mid-1970s, a back-to-basics movement grew up across the nation. States brought in minimum-competency tests in the hope that high-school graduates could at least read, write, and compute at an eighth-grade level. One set of 1970 reading scores showed that 36 percent of the nation's fourth graders could not read a fourth-grade lesson. That percent would change very little over the next decade. What was worse, most fourth graders who could not read at grade level would never get beyond that reading level during the rest of their schooling.

In the twenty years after the Russians launched their Sputnik satellite in 1957, a federal agency called the National Science Foundation (NSF) spent $500 million on curriculum and teacher development. The NSF attempted to bring in new teaching methods, including the New Math. When NSF's efforts seemed to have failed by the late 1970s, Congress canceled most NSF school-related projects.

Even though billions had been spent in these decades, much of American education was failing to educate the students. Parents had a right to be disappointed. One educator of the time said that the failure of the American educational system was the result of public schools not properly teaching children in the first three grades to read and write and to figure with whole numbers.

Others pointed to the distraction in the schools caused by turmoil in society at large and in homes where many parents divorced. The schools were also coping with the largest influx of immigrants since World War I. These immigrants came from all over the world, and most needed to learn English before they could do well in school.

Presidents Kennedy and Johnson had believed that better funding of education would bring an end to poverty. At the end of the 1970s, people were less sure that the schools or government could solve the problems of poverty.

A Troubled Present but Hopeful Future

The American educational system needed much improvement by 1980. In the next decades, the United States would be one of seven nations out of forty in the Western Hemisphere with an adult literacy below 80 percent. The other six were Haiti, Guatemala, Nicaragua, Belize, Honduras, and El Salvador, some of the world's poorest countries.

To turn things around, the federal government and states worked to raise educational standards. New achievement tests were required. Some states considered lengthening the school year. Others raised salaries and requirements for beginning teachers. Graduation standards often became more strict.

Despite all the teaching theories, failed or successful, a good education was acquired by many young Americans. In schools all around the nation, there were dedicated, skillful teachers who could bring out the best in their students. And as in no other nation, U.S. schools offered remarkable "enrichment" programs. These included a wide range of activities and sports that taught valuable lessons. These offered rewarding life experiences that went well beyond the classroom.

Chapter Four

The Economy

Pollution from factory smokestacks (LEFT) **cloud the skies over the south side of Chicago, Illinois; Hennepin Avenue** (RIGHT) **in Minneapolis, Minnesota, in 1973.**
(National Archives)

Americans had good reason to feel optimistic about the future at the start of the 1960s. They were used to the prosperous 1950s, and the Kennedy presidency promised an even better "New Frontier" of opportunity for the country. That New Frontier held challenging difficulties, too, he warned. Yet most of the nation was confident and prepared to meet any challenge.

This New Frontier soon would mean government action to stimulate the economy and increase spending on the military and the space race. The concept of a New Frontier recalled the nation's adventurous past, settling the wilderness and expanding westward. The idea of boldly entering a new era inspired many Americans, especially the youth.

Exciting technologies and inventions appeared everywhere in the 1960s. American manufacturers dominated the economies of the free world, as the noncommunist countries were called. Although most families feared the dangers of the Cold War, the American military was the strongest on earth. There was general peace despite the growing Civil Rights movement that saw occasional street battles and unrest. Among the many advantages to living in America was the low cost of food compared to prices in other developed countries.

With its great wealth and strong civil liberties, the United States was the envy of the world. More Americans than ever could afford to take up international tourism, traveling by air to visit other lands. They brought with them both valuable American dollars and positive American attitudes. By the 1960s, the economy surged, largely thanks to government spending. The Johnson administration approved funding for the War on Poverty, for health care, and for further space exploration. At the same time, the Vietnam War expanded in scope and cost, and military spending grew rapidly.

Cracks opened in the American world image. Many people at home and abroad came to think U.S. involvement in the Vietnam war was wrong. The economy grew too quickly because of too much spending, and prosperity turned into indebtedness. For the first time since World War II, the nation found itself in serious economic difficulty. Too much public debt and rising consumer prices shook American confidence.

Dramatic changes in production technology and the rise of foreign competition in manufacturing made the 1970s an uncertain time. Too many of the nation's factories were growing old. Equipment and manufacturing methods were not as good as new foreign factories.

For certain business sectors, deep troubles came from natural competition and from changing times. For example, newspaper and magazine publishers lost business to broadcast media—radio and television. Advertisers found more and more consumers viewing and listening instead of reading. Long-running publications went out of business. The much-loved *Saturday Evening Post*, a weekly general-interest magazine, stopped publishing in 1969. In 1972, *Life* magazine, famous for its news photography, ceased its weekly publication. Many afternoon newspapers shut down or merged with morning newspapers. By the time the afternoon paper appeared, the news in its pages was stale. Radio and television had already reported much of what the newspaper contained delivered late in the day.

A change in the legal status of young people eighteen to twenty years of age was one of the important milestones of this period. In 1971, Congress passed the twenty-sixth Amendment to the Constitution, lowering the voting age from twenty-one to eighteen. It was said that if young people could serve in the military, they should also have full rights as citizens. Now the government had to pay more attention to opinions of these youngest voters.

For the past two decades, this age group had enjoyed immense spending power as consumers. Now they had the voting power to go with it. An issue of increasing interest to them was the health of the environment.

One potential milestone was virtually ignored: in 1974 Congress passed a law to convert the United States to the metric system of numbering and measurement. At first, road signs began to appear with metric distances and speed limits (kilometers per hour) alongside the traditional "English" miles. Schoolchildren began to learn metric. Labels on cans and bottles stated a product's weight in both ounces and grams. Canada and the United Kingdom did "go metric," but Americans balked. The metric-movement was allowed to die quietly.

A milestone long remembered by those who endured it was the "Gasoline Crisis" of 1973–1974. Heating oil and gasoline shortages made energy prices skyrocket. Long lines of cars waiting for a gas pump were harsh proof that the world was changing. Even the powerful United States could not always control its own economic destiny.

Yet the United States was far wealthier than any other country. One measurement of this was that its consumers owned more than half the world's 200 million telephones. Also, America's inventive genius led the way, as it developed the most advanced electronic and computer technology. From the troubled 1960s and 1970s sprang a technology revolution that would change the world—and change it faster than ever before.

War Profits and Labor Unrest

The beginning of the 1960s saw a sluggish economy and high unemployment. In 1962, the unemployment rate was 5.5 percent, meaning fifty-five people out of every 1,000 could not find a job. This rate was the third highest since the early 1940s. Unemployment stayed high for several years. When involvement in the Vietnam War increased after 1965, military spending pumped billions of dollars into the economy. Industry roared, and employment was high. The unemployment rate dropped to 3.6 percent in 1968. This was the lowest rate since the early 1950s.

For several years, government spending for military needs spurred the American economy. The surge in business brought greater wealth to the middle class. By the end of the 1960s, there were more millionaires than ever. Their spending power stimulated the sale of luxury goods and expensive cars. Investing in the stock market became hot in the 1960s. More than 24 million individuals owned shares by 1978. This was an increase of 40 percent over 1960 and four times 1950's shareholders. Women numbered more than half the individual shareholders.

Traditionally, companies sold shares of stock in order to have cash to buy new equipment or to expand operations. Unfortunately, cash from the sales of shares did not always go toward investing in the company, its factories, or equipment. The income from selling shares too often went to benefit major owners and executives. As a result, U.S. factories were rusting. American industry was less efficient than foreign industry, which used the latest and best equipment. America found itself poorly equipped to compete with more modern industrial methods.

When plans were introduced to improve manufacturing methods, labor unions often opposed them. Unions feared they would lose jobs to new technology such as robots on assembly lines. In 1970, many industries around the country lost business when thousands of autoworkers struck General Motors, the largest car maker. The autoworkers' walkout lasted sixty-seven days before the union and company reached a settlement. This was more proof that labor unions were strong and had a potent effect on the economy.

Also in 1970, the postal workers union went on strike. This crippled the nation's mail service and hurt the economy. The post office was crucial to America's business. Postal workers went back on the job only after they won concessions from their employer, the federal government. Whatever benefits the postal workers gained, it was generally thought that the post office itself was inefficient. In 1963, the first zip codes had been introduced. This greatly sped up the sorting and delivery of mail. The quantity of mail was enormous, however. In the late 1970s, the post office handled more than 80 billion pieces of mail a year.

Strong competition for mail-delivery appeared by the 1970s. Private, regional express-delivery companies were consolidating into nationwide carriers, such as Federal Express and United Parcel Service. Many consumers preferred the convenience and efficiency of the private express companies. These companies became immensely successful delivering packages and mail more quickly and directly than the government post office.

In general, union members earned very good wages. Most blue-collar workers who were "unionized" could afford nice homes and new cars. Prosperous union workers were an important segment of the consumer economy. Yet labor union demands for more pay drove up business costs. Their strikes disrupted production. To avoid the high expense and the work stoppages of unions, many manufacturers moved to other parts of the country. In the South, for example, most workers were not unionized. They could be hired for much less.

In the older manufacturing cities, unions lost thousands of jobs in this period. At the same time, they also lost respect because of corruption among their top leaders. As a result, union membership steadily declined, as did their power. By 1980, the total work stoppages were less than half of 1970's stoppages. With the decline of the union went much of the blue-collar worker's political influence and spending power.

Not all unions were declining, however. Recently unionized migrant farmworkers reversed the antiunion trend. California migrant workers fought successfully for better working conditions.

A Time of Doubt

The nation's booming prosperity in the late 1960s did not last into the 1970s. Wartime spending drained the federal treasury. Spending for "War on Poverty" programs also cost the government heavily. The antipoverty programs helped narrow the gap between rich and poor, raising the nation's overall standard of living. Yet, all this spending dramatically increased the public debt—money borrowed by the national government. The public debt was $313.8 billion in 1965, at the start of the Vietnam War. It had risen to $533.2 billion by war's end in 1975.

All this borrowing and spending put a tremendous strain on the economy. In part, this was because the government was borrowing so much that there was not enough money available for businesses to borrow. Whenever less money is available, it becomes more expensive to borrow. Then the cost of borrowing—the interest rate—goes up. In turn, this rise in interest rates makes it more costly to do business. Everything then costs more.

When goods become more expensive—meaning more dollars are needed to buy them—then the dollar has less value. That requires employers to pay their employees more to keep up with rising costs. And the more money that is in circulation, the more things will cost. This makes the dollar worth even less. Such an upward spiral in costs is termed *inflation*.

So even though people were earning more money in the 1970s, they needed more to live. Consumer goods cost more, as did rent, housing, and electricity. In 1965, per capita personal income was $2,773 a year. That figure more than doubled by 1975 to $5,851. This rise in personal income did not necessarily mean consumers could buy more, however. Costs had gone up as rapidly as income. For example, the cost of food doubled between 1960 and 1975, and clothing went up about 40 percent, as did the cost of electricity.

The American consumer felt the financial pinch. Use to low costs and high wages, Americans found their way of life undermined by inflation. The population worried about the future economy. Would there be another Great Depression? In 1971, President Nixon imposed a ninety-day freeze on wages and prices. Employers were not allowed to raise salaries, and stores could not raise their prices. Nixon hoped to slow down inflation, but it was highly unusual for the federal government to regulate wages and prices. Still, most Americans accepted such a drastic step as being good for the country. They wanted to try anything to improve the economy. Labor unions did object loudly, but there was nothing they could do about the freeze.

Nixon's policy did little to slow inflation, however. The economy remained weak and unstable for the next few years. Inflation continued, so that in 1973 Nixon ordered a temporary freeze on all retail food prices. Among the most troubling increases in price was the rising cost of oil and gasoline.

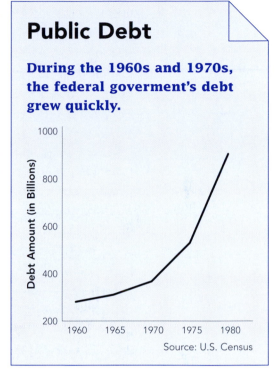

Public Debt

During the 1960s and 1970s, the federal goverment's debt grew quickly.

Debt Amount (in Billions)

Source: U.S. Census

Oil Consumption and the Gas Crisis

Between 1960 and 1980, fuel-oil prices went up six times higher. Gasoline prices also rose drastically. From 1920 through 1965, the price of gasoline had been between twenty and thirty cents per gallon. It then surged to 35.7 cents per gallon by 1970. Much higher prices were yet to come. Over the next decade, the price of gasoline more than tripled, rising to $1.35 per gallon.

The United States was the world's leading consumer of energy, whether from oil, coal, or gas. At the same time, many new goods and products were being made from petroleum (oil), further increasing its consumption. Petroleum-based goods ranged from hard plastic containers to polyurethane sheeting and polyester clothing. Oil was essential to the life of the American consumer. Its rising price warned there was less of it to go around. Much of America's oil came from foreign countries.

The exciting discovery of vast fields of oil in Alaska during the late 1960s gave the nation new hope. The Alaskan oil field was twice as large as any other in North America. At a cost of $7.7 billion, the 800-mile-long Trans-Alaska pipeline was built to bring the oil to a seaport for shipment. The pipeline went into operation in 1977. It was thought this would make the country independent from foreign oil. It would not be enough, however.

By 1980, Americans consumed almost one-fourth of all the energy produced in the world that year. The United States produced two-thirds of the oil it used, but it depended on other countries for the remaining one-third. Most of that imported oil came from the Arab nations of the Middle East. In 1973, Arab oil states stopped exporting oil for several months. They were angry with the United States for supporting Israel, with whom they had just fought a war. Middle Eastern oil was temporarily cut off to the United States—"embargoed." The embargo created a shortage. This made oil prices shoot up and caused panic across the nation.

Service stations ran out of gasoline. Fuel oil was in short supply. Prices for petroleum-based consumer products went up 12 percent in 1974. Business and industry costs rose, and the American economy suffered. Since the United States was the biggest market for goods and products from the rest of the world, many other countries also suffered. Critics said that gasoline producers intentionally took advantage of the shortage of oil. They withheld gasoline from the American market or reduced their production of gasoline. In this way, they made immense profits from the gasoline they did sell.

The Gas Crisis of 1973 and 1974 led to long lines at the gas station and limits to the amount of gas drivers could buy at one time.
(Library of Congress)

This was known as the Gas Crisis of 1973–1974. During the worst weeks of the crisis, many drivers got up in the middle of the night to be first in line at the gas pumps. They waited for hours for the station to open, hoping it would have a supply of gas. Harried station owners pumped gasoline until they ran out. Then they had to tell the bad news to the unfortunate people still waiting in line. Often station owners announced they would only sell to regular customers.

Some consumers filled up extra gasoline containers and stored them in their homes or in the trunks of cars. Storing highly explosive gasoline in random containers was dangerous. Some cars burst into flames when a can of extra gas in the trunk exploded.

Since most American cars were large, with low gas mileage, consumers had to cut down their driving. Leisure trips by car were drastically reduced. This caused a decline in regional tourism that hurt the economy even more. It was a time of uncertainty and doubt. Many Americans feared things would get even worse.

During his term in office, 1976–1980, President Jimmy Carter tried to promote sources of energy other than oil and coal. He established a government policy to support the development of solar and wind power. The government funded pioneering research into these fields. Carter received little support from Congress, however. The oil companies were politically powerful. They were not in favor of alternative power sources.

When Carter asked the American people to reduce their personal consumption of oil and gasoline, again he found little enthusiasm. One major consumer attitude was changing, however: Americans began to drive smaller, more fuel-efficient cars.

By 1980, the trend toward smaller cars was in full swing. Even the major automakers were responding to consumer demands, and 40 percent of American auto production was compact cars. Yet small imported foreign cars made a powerful impact on the auto industry. Japanese and European cars took approximately 18 percent of the American market. Many consumers considered foreign cars to be of much higher quality than most American-made autos.

To keep up with foreigners, American manufacturing still needed to improve its plants, equipment, training, and methods.

A New Speed Limit

In January 1974, President Nixon signed a new law that lowered the national speed limit from 65 to 55 miles per hour. This slower speed made most automobiles more efficient and so cut down on gas consumption. It also was a safer speed for highway driving. The 55-miles-per-hour speed limit saved lives. Although the annual deaths from motor-vehicle accidents rose steadily, the number of cars on the roads increased much faster than the death rate. Almost 46,000 Americans were killed in car accidents in 1975, and more than 53,000 in 1980, a rise of 15 percent. Passenger cars numbered almost 89.3 million in 1970, rising to 121.7 million in 1980, almost 30 percent more.

New Delights and Home Entertainment

In other fields, such as electronics and home entertainment, inventive developments set the course of the future.

The travel industry became immediately more efficient in 1962, when American Airlines established a system for making reservations simpler. Called SABER, it linked thousands of travel agencies with airline reservation terminals and ticket desks. This took much of the headache out of finding the best flight to a destination.

"Faster" was the watchword of organizing data and information during these decades. "Data processing," which once had to do with compiling numbers from punch cards and spewing out perforated paper tape, added the function of "word processing."

First came innovations in recording and home entertainment. The audiocassette, developed in the Netherlands, arrived in the United States in 1963. Cassettes were more portable and sturdier than vinyl records that were fragile and scratched too easily. A few years later, in 1967, recorded music improved in quality when Dolby technology eliminated "audio hiss." Now stereo sound systems offered unsurpassed tone and clarity. Consumers were enthusiastic about the immense variety of recorded music. Sales of records and tapes reached an all-time high of $683 million in 1979. In this same year, the Sony Walkman was introduced, and recorded music was more portable than ever.

Television was by far the most popular home entertainment. It received a major boost with the arrival of the video-recording system in 1975. Videocassette recorders (VCRs) were expensive at first, costing more than $2,200 as part of a package that included a television. By 1980, VCRs were sold separately, and their prices were dropping. Americans quickly adopted the VCR for recording television shows. Watching rented videocassettes of movies soon became the most popular use of VCRs. Television viewing expanded further in the mid-1970s, when satellites started to deliver programming nationwide.

Video games took their first step in 1972, with the invention of "Pong." This was electronic ping-pong played on a home television screen. Video games were off and running, becoming increasingly complex, and were too often violent. But their vast popularity with children was unstoppable. Atari, the best-known game producer, started its marketing push in 1975. Atari games used control boxes that converted the screen into an electronic playing field. Hockey and tennis were early versions. In 1976, $250 million worth of video games were sold. In the next few years, pay-to-play video games were everywhere in public places, from shopping centers to restaurants. "Video arcades" opened up, offering many varieties of games. Arcades became a gathering place for young people, who spent their time and money playing for hours.

Other technological improvements were great successes with consumers. These included the automatically focusing Polaroid camera, which appeared in 1972. Amateur photography had never been easier or as popular. By the end of the decade, 35-millimeter cameras automatically loaded film, focused, and set the exposure.

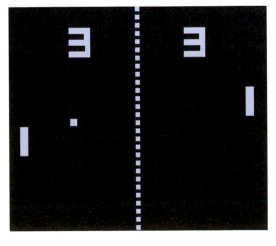

The first video games appeared in the mid-1970s. Pong, shown here, was a form of electronic ping-pong. (Courtesy of Jim Burmester)

Another major development was the soft contact lens. The Food and Drug Administration approved the use of contact lenses for the first time in 1971. This was a major innovation in eye care, as well as in fashion. Contact lenses were immediately popular with those who wanted to get rid of their eyeglasses for at least part of the day.

The 1970s ended with the introduction of an item that became indispensable in homes, schools, and offices. The 3M Company's "Post-it" note stuck to almost anything and came off without damaging the surface.

Approaching the Computer Age

Work in offices and schools was much easier after 1960, thanks to the introduction that year of the Xerox photocopying machine. In the past, copies—or duplicates—had been made with carbon paper or on "mimeograph" machines. Mimeographs used ink and a drum roller to duplicate a stencil of the original document. The process was slow and messy, the duplicate usually fuzzy and unclear. The Xerox copier was a photographic process, clean and fast. The Xerox company added to its success by bringing out the Telecopier, a fax machine, in 1966.

International Business Machines (IBM) produced a popular electric typewriter in 1961, called the Selectric. Typewriters were manually operated and had no memory, as computers do. IBM's electric typewriters improved steadily, but they were doomed to be overtaken by word processors. The first word processors were like computerized typewriters with the ability to store large amounts of data. IBM had developed an early word processor by 1964 but did not offer it as a replacement for the profitable Selectric typewriter.

Sixties innovations in office equipment paved the way for the appearance of the "Wang 1200" in 1971. This was the first word processor to go on the market. By 1974, word processors had begun to replace typewriters. In less than ten years, typewriters would be completely outmoded.

In the 1970s, computerization transformed every field of business and production, from accounting to typesetting to mechanics. At first, the most prominent personal computers were hand-held calculators. In 1961, Texas Instruments patented the "silicon chip," a miniature electronic circuit that eliminated the

need for complex wiring. The chip made it possible for computers to compute more and do it at lightning speed. At the same time, computers were becoming ever smaller.

Other pioneering computer technology and designs were in the works. By the late 1970s, the large mainframe computer was at the heart of most computing operations. This was one central computer connected to a system of individual workstations. The workstations were organized into a network that shared the mainframe. Operators sitting at workstations communicated with the mainframe to carry out computing tasks. IBM took the lead in developing a "personal computer" that could operate without linking to a central mainframe. For all IBM's success, the company soon would run into stiff competition from computer geniuses working to create new models.

General use of personal computers was still a decade away when math genius Bill Gates dropped out of Harvard in 1974 to write software—operating programs—for computers. The following year, Gates established a company called Microsoft. It would be a while before Microsoft could match IBM's corporate wealth and power, but Gates was destined to be the most successful computer entrepreneur of all.

Before the 1960s, computers were extremely large. This IBM system from the mid-1960s took up much of a room.
(Library of Congress)

Steve Wozniak and Steve Jobs, founders of Apple Computer, with the hard drive of one of their early computers. (Courtesy of Apple Computers, Inc.)

In 1976, partners Steven Wozniak and Steven Jobs finally finished building the Apple I Computer in the Jobs's family garage. The computer's initial price was $666.66, and it had eight bytes of RAM (random access memory). Apple Computers would go on to become a leading manufacturer of computers and creator of innovative software.

Government Action for Consumers and Environment

Medical care, drugs, and nursing services were a fast-growing cost to consumers in this time. At first, the government gave little financial support to those who had trouble paying their medical costs. The elderly were especially in difficulty, and there was widespread poverty among them.

Before 1965, only government employers and private businesses offered health insurance for their employees. Many Americans, especially the aged, had little or no health insurance. To remedy this situation, the federal government created Medicare in 1965. This program helped to pay for health care for the elderly. The high cost of medicine, hospitalization, and treatment was finally lowered for older Americans.

New attitudes to personal health developed during the 1960s and 1970s. Younger people, in particular, were increasingly conscious of what they were eating. The health-food movement began to grow, especially in California and in college communities. Those who wanted to consume wholesome, or natural, food shopped for products that were as natural as possible. They avoided food that had chemical additives or preservatives. They also avoided processed foods and foods that had lost much nutritional value by being packaged for store shelves. The health-food movement grew steadily in these decades, but many Americans still smoked.

In 1966, the Surgeon General required that tobacco companies place a warning on cigarette packs, saying, "Caution: Smoking may be hazardous to your health." More than 13 million Americans stopped smoking between 1966 and 1970. By the early 1970s, many older Americans were giving up cigarettes while many young people were starting to smoke. Clever advertising pushed smoking as cool and sexy. The tobacco industry stoutly denied that there was any evidence of smoking being addictive.

The federal government did not yet take a stand about addiction, but it did oppose tobacco advertising that could be seen by young people. In 1971, television and radio broadcasters banned cigarette advertising. Cigarette ads continued in print advertising such as newspapers, magazines, and billboards. In 1972, the Surgeon General reported for the first time about the dangers of "sidestream" (or secondhand) smoke. Still, tobacco sales remained strong.

Consumerism found its place in the rising interest in environmentalism. For example, many Americans wanted their food to be free of the pesticides and chemicals used in commercial agriculture. They bought products that guaranteed this, even if they were more expensive. Also, increasing numbers of Americans wanted automobiles to be more efficient and cut down on carbon monoxide emissions. For many, their car preference depended not on stylish looks but on high gas mileage and improved emission controls.

The nation's intensifying interest in the environment was proven on April 21, 1970, when the first Earth Day was celebrated. This festivity made the statement that the environment must be protected. Earth Day grew larger every year and is now celebrated around the world.

Also in 1970, the federal Environmental Protection Agency (EPA) was established. The EPA had broad powers to regulate pollution and toxic waste. It grew to become one of the most powerful agencies in the government. In this same year, the federal government passed the Clean Air Act, requiring automakers to build engines with reduced emissions. Because of consumer demands, the federal government also began to develop new standards of automobile safety.

In the following decades, the government would play an even stronger role in regulating consumer goods, conserving natural resources, and protecting the environment.

This button promotes environmental protection. (private collection)

Chapter Five

Work

An employee at the 3M Company in New Ulm, Minnesota (LEFT) works on one of the company's products; morning rush hour (RIGHT) in New York City (National Archives)

In contrast to the prosperous years after World War II, the American economy was sluggish in the early 1960s. Following several economic recessions in the 1950s, unemployment was high. Then came the Unites States' involvement in the Vietnam War, beginning in 1964. The economy grew rapidly as the government spent a large amount of money to support the war effort, and employment increased. By the 1970s, this spending later became a financial drain that brought about difficult economic times.

The 1960s and 1970s were also a time of great change for women and minorities in the workplace. Laws were passed to limit discrimination against these groups. While some challenges still remained by the end of the period, the era opened up new opportunities for many of those who had previously been denied them.

The Military, High Tech, and the Environment

In the course of the Vietnam War, the military became a major employer. More than 11 million young men and women joined the armed forces. Although the military did not pay well, it often provided educational opportunities. Some servicemen and women might learn management skills, and others become technicians in electronics, for example. Some were trained as flight controllers for planes landing and taking off. Others learned to pilot cargo-carrying aircraft. Skills such as navigation, engine maintenance, and communication could lead to good jobs after the service. Many in the military learned to program and operate computers, which were increasingly important to military technology and the space race.

Foreign Competition and the "Rust Belt"

Through the 1960s, America's industrial base was shrinking. Manufacturing was busy during the Vietnam War, but foreign competition became stronger every year. American industry paid its workers higher wages and benefits than what most foreign competitors paid. In some industries, such as textiles, foreign workers earned almost nothing compared to Americans. Lower salaries made foreign goods cheaper to produce.

The cost of doing business in the United States was usually much higher than in foreign countries. At the same time, the quality of American goods was often not as good as foreign goods. For instance, excellent Japanese and German automobiles and Swedish steel won increasing numbers of customers in the United States. Prosperity after World War II had led to complacency in many American industries. One of the slowest to change its ways was automobile manufacturing.

By the early 1970s, most American cars seemed big and clumsy compared to compact Japanese or German cars. American autos were sleek, luxurious, and air-conditioned, while foreign vehicles were simple and practical. Many Americans preferred sensible foreign cars over glitzy American gas-guzzlers. Foreign compacts such as Honda, Datsun, and Volkswagen were extremely fuel-efficient. This key difference became all too obvious in the gasoline crises of the 1970s.

American autoworkers, as much as consumers, wanted new designs and better-made vehicles. For autoworkers, it was a matter of pride that an American-made car should be just as well-made as the foreign competition. The Ford Mustang, introduced in 1965, was one answer. The Mustang was sporty, fuel-efficient, and relatively inexpensive. As more good medium-sized and compact cars began to roll off U.S. assembly lines, autoworkers and dealers felt a new sense of hope. They believed the United States would hold on to world leadership in their industry. Still, foreign automobiles kept improving as well.

Great American Construction Projects

The 1960s and 1970s saw the completion of some of America's most important construction projects. Despite economic uncertainty, architects and builders succeeded brilliantly with these projects. Workers at every level collaborated to create these wonders of American commerce, trade, and travel. Power plants and dams prepared the way for cities to be built and for agriculture to thrive.

New York City's World Trade Center, with its Twin Towers, was dedicated in 1973. It stood 110 stories high (1,350 feet) and contained more than 9 million square feet of office space. The World Trade Center became the center of New York's—and America's—financial commerce. It was the city's pride and a symbol of American leadership in international business. When completed, the World Trade Center was the world's tallest building—but not for long.

Later in 1973, the Sears Tower was completed in Chicago. It rose 110 floors (1,454 feet), and became the world's tallest building. While the World Trade Center was faced in white, the Sears Tower was sheathed in black aluminum and bronze-tinted glass.

Another of America's most impressive construction achievements in this period was also in New York. The Verrazano-Narrows Bridge, crossing Lower New York Bay, was completed in 1964. The bridge had a span of more than 4,200 feet and was one of the longest in the world. Several other great bridges went into service in this period, including the 2,150-foot-long Delaware River Bridge in 1968 and the 1,800-foot East River Bridge in New York City, in 1961.

In 1968, California could boast one of the world's highest dams, as the Oroville Dam in Featherville was completed. Oroville was 770 feet high and the fourth highest in the world at the time. The world's largest dam was completed at New Cornelia Tailings in Arizona in 1973, with a volume of 274,000 cubic yards.

Other great American construction projects of the time included several of the world's largest hydroelectric plants. The John Day Dam in Oregon-Washington had the fifth-largest electric production capacity in the world when it was built in 1969. This plant could produce 2,700 megawatts of electricity.

Despite the events of the turbulent 1960s and 1970s, American workers built many projects that were among the greatest achievements in the world.

New York's World Trade Center under construction (Port Authority of New York New Jersey)

As the American auto industry struggled, foreign automobiles won 20 percent of the American market by the mid-1970s. The result was a decline in American auto companies. Fewer cars were built, and many jobs were lost.

For decades, Americans had enjoyed the highest standard of living in the world. In the 1970s, the country dropped to tenth place. With inflation high, above 12 percent, increasing salaries and wages could not keep pace with rising prices.

Raw materials, such as crops, timber, iron ore, and minerals, were still exported. But an increasing quantity of manufactured products from cars to electronics to steel were imported. America's manufacturing output was weakening. Once-roaring factories of the Midwest closed, never to reopen. Many industries moved away to nonunion states, and others moved their production abroad. The region from western New York to western Michigan had been called America's "industrial belt." Now, however, its warehouses were empty, its assembly lines being shut down. Factories stood silent. Their deteriorating machinery would not run again. The new name for this region was the "rust belt."

Farmworkers Unionize

Labor unions continued their steady decline in membership and in political power. In this time of industrial slackening and job loss, one of the few successes for unions was the increase in women members. Women formed their own associations to speak for themselves. The National Association for Working Women and the Coalition of Labor Union Women were the main groups.

Another notable success for trade unions in this time was the unionization of government workers. As governments at every level, local to federal, had increased in size, their employees had organized unions. Public employee unions included "white-collar" government office workers, "blue-collar" maintenance staffs, teachers, postal workers, police, and firefighters. In the early 1970s, their membership rose to 4 million. In 1970, postal workers went on strike for the first time in history, causing major disruptions. The army had to deliver the mail until the strike was resolved. The power of public-employees unions was now firmly established.

Another workers' organization went against the trend of decline: the United Farm Workers (UFW) union. The union was

César Chávez
(Library of Congress)

established by César Chávez in the 1960s. Spanish-speaking migrant workers, who had been unrepresented, flocked to the union. Major operators of corporate farms strongly opposed the UFW. They warned workers that they would be fired if they tried to join the union. Working conditions for migrant farmworkers were so miserable, however, that thousands defied their bosses. For one thing, they objected to laboring in the fields morning to night without proper meals or rest breaks.

Many large agricultural operations did not even offer farmworkers decent toilet facilities. This meant that these workers had to relieve themselves in the fields, with nowhere to wash their hands before returning to work. Chávez and his supporters among civil rights groups and other unions publicized such unhealthy conditions. American consumers began to realize that they, too, might be threatened by unsanitary standards in the fields. The UFW assumed a strong moral position in their campaign for basic workers' rights. They went on strike and picketed. They called for public boycotts of lettuce and grapes.

Widespread popular support was behind the UFW. Many Americans refused to buy California grapes until a major labor dispute was settled. Vineyard owners were among the strongest early opponents of the UFW. In time, however, the grape boycott turned the tide. Grape growers gave up their resistance, and Chávez won a major victory. The UFW won higher wages, health insurance, and safer working conditions.

Women at Work

As the economy grew during the 1960s, the demand for workers helped to open up new opportunities for women. Young women of the baby boom generation were entering the work force in large numbers. The government's affirmative-action policies helped women and minorities acquire jobs and training. Women began to work in positions that until then had been considered unfeminine. For example, they became miners and heavy equipment operators. Until the 1970s, even women service-station attendants, pumping gas, were rare.

Many women were trained to assume management jobs that once had gone only to men. Some argued that women should remain at home and let the men take the best jobs.

Further controversy developed as women demanded equal

pay for equal work. In 1963, President Kennedy formed a commission to study the issue. The Commission on Women reported that females suffered discrimination in the workplace. After this report, all fifty states established their own commissions to look into the status of women. Soon after the Kennedy commission report appeared, Congress passed the Equal Pay Act of 1963. This act required that women be paid the same as men for doing the same work. This was a major breakthrough to overcoming unequal treatment of women workers. The following year's Civil Rights Act further strengthened women's rights. It prohibited discrimination on the basis of either gender and race.

Despite these laws, it was still difficult for women to get ahead and almost impossible for a woman to rise to the highest levels of management. Often no one in a company openly discussed the limitations that faced women. Prejudice against women directing men, for example, might not be voiced in the corporation's daily operations. Yet that prejudice was there, though it was invisible. These limitations were like a glass ceiling that prevented women from rising any higher. The term *glass ceiling* would come into wide use in the 1980s. Unspoken limitations to women's advancement in the workplace helped bring about the modern women's liberation movement.

In 1960, women's wages and salaries were 30.9 percent of those of men. This was a dramatic decline from 45.6 percent in

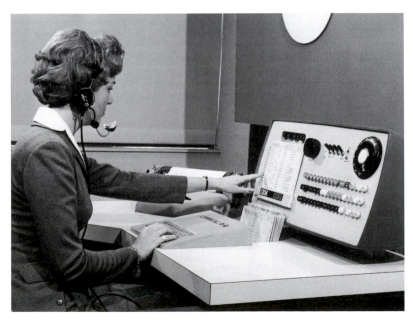

A woman wearing a headset operates an early-generation IBM desktop computer in an office. (Getty Archives)

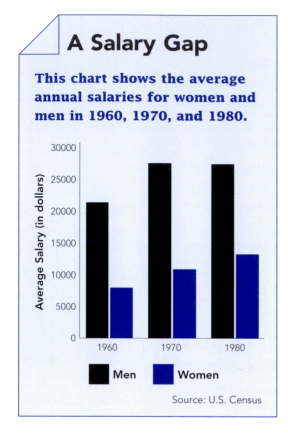

A Salary Gap

This chart shows the average annual salaries for women and men in 1960, 1970, and 1980.

Men ■   Women ■

Source: U.S. Census

1947, which was the highest percent until late in the twentieth century. In 1970, women wage earners took home only 33.5 percent of what men earned. That figure was 39.3 percent in 1980. Women's wages and salaries were on a steady rise, though. They gained in percent of men's wages in almost every year for the rest of the twentieth century.

Government statistics showed an increase in the number of women earning wages or salaries between 1960 and 1980. In 1960, they numbered almost 26 million. They grew to more than 36.7 million in 1970 and more than 49.32 million by 1980. Men earning wages or salaries numbered approximately 43.3 million in 1960. They were more than 52.2 million in 1970 and more than 60.1 million in 1980. In each decade, women employees increased as a percent of the total workforce.

Incomes showed a great difference between men and women employees in this period. But that difference began to narrow. In 1960, men with wages or salaries earned a median of $21,433. That year, women earned a median income of $7,950. In 1970, men earned $27,623 and women $10,885. In 1980, men earned $27,480 and women $13,269.

Women's achievements and rights received international attention in 1975, which the United Nations declared the International Year of the Woman. This declaration was intended both to honor women and to broaden awareness of the challenges and inequalities they faced.

Affirmative Action and Discrimination

The 1964 Civil Rights Act made racial discrimination in the workplace illegal. The next year, an executive order by President Johnson took that one step further. It required all businesses and institutions that did work for the federal government or with federal funds to help make up for the harm done by years of past discrimination. This policy was known as affirmative action. Some schools and businesses gave preference to candidates of racial minorities. Others created quotas for the number of candidates from several different minority groups. In 1972, affirmative action was extended to women.

African Americans, Hispanic Americans, Asian Americans, Native Americans, and women could now find jobs or attend schools, they might not have previously. But there were complaints that this created "reverse discrimination" against non-Hispanic white male candidates. In 1978, the Supreme Court ruled in the case of *Bakke v. University of California* that the university could not set aside quotas for minority candidates. But it did say that race could be considered as a factor in admissions. Affirmative action continued to be debated throughout the century.

By the 1970s, new political activists promoted their own antidiscrimination movements. One of the strongest movements fought to protect the rights of older Americans. Many Americans found that before they reached the retirement age of 65, their employers would fire them and replace them with a younger, lower-paid worker. The American Association of Retired Persons (AARP) opposed this form of discrimination based on age. They became a powerful lobbying group for Americans above the age of fifty. The AARP organized a successful march on Washington in 1973.

Gay and lesbian activists called for an end to discrimination based on sexual preference. This group was galvanized by the 1969 police raid on a Greenwich Village gay bar known as the Stonewall Inn. Patrons fought with the police, and the result was a riot. The clash was one of several that year. Gays and lesbians defied the authorities who had the power to prosecute them for breaking laws that forbid sexual activity between same-sex partners.

Demands to end discrimination with regard to age and sexual preference began to change the workplace. In the following decades, these movements would have great success. The laws of the nation would be changed to respect and recognize everyone's human rights, including their right to work.

The median family income continued to increase. In 1960, it was $28,013. By 1970, it had increased to $38,345 and by 1980 to $40,999.

At the bottom of the income scale were those Americans in

poverty. In 1960, a family of four was in poverty if it earned less than $3,022 a year. The poverty level for a family of that size was $3,986 in 1970 and $8,414 in 1980. In 1968, 13 percent of Americans lived below the poverty line, compared with 20 percent in 1960. Things were improving for the poor, thanks to the Johnson administration's War on Poverty. For middle-class workers in the 1970s, though, jobs and earnings were becoming ever more uncertain.

Better Pay Buys Less

Incomes rose in the 1960s and 1970s, but inflation rose too. Inflation is a decrease in the value of money. It limits the buying power of a worker's paycheck, even when more dollars are being earned.

In order to make sure employees earn enough to live on, the federal government requires employers to pay a minimum hourly wage. Although not all members of Congress agree with increasing the minimum wage, Congress generally has increased the wage every few years to keep up with inflation.

The nation suffered through several major and minor recessions between 1960 and 1980. Recessions are downturns, when business, production, and employment weaken. One of the most serious recessions of this era lasted from April 1960 to February 1961. In some ways, this recession marked an end to the prosperity that followed World War II. The next two recessions were marked by inflation brought about by the Vietnam War.

In 1974, the economy slumped into the worst recession in forty years. Unemployment rose to 8.3 percent in 1975, 3 percent higher than four years earlier. This percent represented almost 8 million people out of work. Like unemployment figures, sales of cars and trucks are often indicators of the nation's economic health. In 1973, more than 14.47 million cars and trucks were sold. But in 1974, it dropped back to 11.54 million.

The Incredible Shrinking Dollar

In 1960, the minimum wage was $1.25 an hour, worth $6.54 in the spending power of 1997 dollars. In 1968, the minimum wage was $1.60, worth $7.36 in 1997 dollars. In terms of spending power, 1968 had the highest minimum wage of the twentieth century. In 1979, the minimum wage rose to $2.90 but was worth only $6.39 in 1997 dollars, a drop of fifteen cents. This meant the minimum hourly wage was worth less in 1979 than it had been in 1960.

The Otte family on
their farm near
Grafton, Nebraska
(National Archives)

The Family Farm

Early in the twentieth century, more than 21 percent of Americans were employed in agriculture. It was a symbol of the nation's health and strength. By 1960, however, only a little more than 8 percent of Americans were in farming. That figure kept falling. In 1980, just above 3 percent of American workers were employed in farming.

The number of American farms also decreased each year. At the same time, their size increased. The growing size of farms was the result of family farms being sold, either to neighboring farmers or to corporate agribusiness. Farms were becoming bigger because corporations could operate them with the most modern machinery and more efficient cultivation methods. Single-family farms had limited amounts of labor, time, and money. A large corporation, on the other hand, had almost unlimited funds to hire employees; erect buildings; buy equipment, livestock, and seed; and get the crops or produce to market for top prices.

Many farmers failed in this period, no matter how hard and long they worked. Yet American agricultural production boomed in this same period. In 1960, for example, the United States exported $4.5 billion in agricultural products. That figure increased to $40.5 billion in 1980. The most successful and profitable farming operations were the agribusiness corporations. These often belonged to giant food-processing companies or to international conglomerates. Such conglomerates included many different kinds of operations from agriculture to pharmaceuticals.

New Computer Jobs

The first PC, or personal computer, was developed in 1962 for use by a scientific researcher. It cost $43,000. Computers had a long way to go before they could appeal to average consumers. Most were large and costly. Yet they were coming into wider use by institutions. In 1964, there were 17,000 computers in the United States, compared with fifteen in 1954. The stage was set for future growth and development in 1969. That was when the federal government began to experiment with linking researchers to computer centers. This allowed them to share hardware and software. It was the first phase of what, in less than twenty years, would become the Internet.

Before 1971, computers and the computerization of business functions were still largely in the dreaming stages. Data processing mainly involved punch cards and magnetic tapes to store information. This required, in turn, the storing and handling of the cards and tapes. It was in 1971 that Intel Corporation of California released a "microprocessor" with the ability to process enormous quantities of data. Creating a silicon chip containing a minute electronic circuit, Intel revolutionized the computer industry. Computer design, manufacturing, and practical use entered a new age, promising great appeal to business and industry. Many startup firms established themselves in the twenty-five miles between Palo Alto and San Jose, California. This region became known as Silicon Valley, named for the silicon chip so important in creating the new industry.

The computer industry exploded in the late 1970s. By the end of the decade, personal computers were making the home office possible. Employees or self-employed individuals who used computers could do their jobs at home. Their work was transferred to a five-inch floppy disk and brought to a central office. There it was loaded into a company computer for others to work with, as needed.

Computers soon became indispensable to business operations. They controlled a company's inventory and ran its equipment, improved its accounting system, and evaluated customer preferences and economic trends.

This demand for computers created millions of jobs, ranging from the manufacture of hardware and the writing of programs to the construction of office space for new companies. Employment opportunities opened up for computer operators, maintenance specialists, and sales staff. Schools began to teach computer basics, programming, and operations. By 1980, the computer industry had provided an essential tool to revolutionize virtually every aspect of American employment, work, and production. The workplace would never be the same.

Environmental Science

The first Earth Day was celebrated in 1970, symbolizing the growing power of the environmentalist movement. On that day across the country were parades, demonstrations, and rallies in favor of protecting the environment and its ecology.

At the time of the first Earth Day, many lawmakers were struggling with how to solve air and water pollution, conserve natural resources, and protect the environment. For advice, they turned to an emerging group of ecologists who had been scientifically trained to study and understand environmental matters. These specialists came out of recently established environmental courses in colleges and universities.

Because of pollution and overpopulation, communities, states, and the federal government all were being forced to address environmental issues. This helped the science of ecology grow. Ecologists studied the natural balance of specific areas. They could often explain what was needed to preserve an area or develop its resources properly. Ecologists became important advisors to governments and

An environmental scientist examines results of an air-pollution analysis. (National Archives)

businesses. For example, metropolitan areas were suffering from severe traffic congestion. Leaders wondered how new highways would affect an area's ecology. They also wanted to know whether pollution would find its way to the drinking water or how would wildlife and plants be affected by new construction.

Ecologists were asked to study the ecology of a building site and offer advice, which government authorities did not always want to follow. If the impact on an area would be unnecessarily damaging, then ecologists suggested changing the plans or even abandoning a project altogether. This created conflicts that were often resolved in court.

The National Environmental Policy Act of 1969 established the federal Environmental Protection Agency (EPA). This act set up a governmental organization to protect and manage the environment. The EPA had to evaluate the many clashes between business and industry on the one hand and environmentalists on the other. For example, loggers, miners, and oil drillers needed to extract nature's resources. Environmentalists demanded that they do so with utmost care. Taking care almost always cost more and took longer than customary methods.

Such disputes brought the interests of business into conflict with the need to preserve nature and its resources. In the middle were the EPA and the ecologists, trying to offer answers to emotional and controversial questions. At stake was not only America's health and natural resources but also the destiny of unborn generations. As the 1980s approached, the two worlds of computers and ecology attracted some of America's finest minds.

Chapter Six

Religion

Religion remained essential to American life and culture between 1960 and 1980, but it was rapidly changing. In the past, most worshippers had accepted religious doctrine, or teaching, as the truth. Now, many were challenging those doctrines. Some inquired deeply in order to understand doctrine better. Others left their faiths completely.

Those who left their mainstream churches and synagogues had plenty of other choices. Never before had the United States known so many religions and beliefs. Millions of Americans took up meditation or explored New Age spirituality, based on ancient lore and mysticism. Thousands of formerly Protestant African Americans turned to Islam. After the federal government lifted restrictions on immigration in the mid-1960s, thousands of new-comers arrived from Latin America and Asia. Some Latin Americans practiced Catholicism with an African influence. Asians brought over several forms of Islam, Buddhism, and Hinduism.

A growing number of worshipers tried to persuade their congregations to be active in social issues. As it did in the broader society, this caused much controversy as people debated what positions to take. The Civil Rights movement, the war in Vietnam, abortion, and the ordination of women created painful divisions.

Religions were being constantly transformed in the 1960s

The Gipson family (LEFT) **of Gruetli, Tennessee say a prayer before their evening meal.** (National Archives) **Members of the Hare Krishna movement** (RIGHT), **an offshoot of the Hindu religion, chant and dance in Minneapolis to raise money for their sect.** (© Bettmann/CORBIS) and 1970s. Worshipers eagerly took part in interfaith dialogues with members of other religions. Many congregations changed their services. They might, for example, substitute guitar music for that of an organ or sing newly composed hymns rather than traditional ones. Roman Catholic masses were offered in English or Spanish, rather than the traditional Latin. Taken together, these new ways of worship further enriched American religious culture.

Religious Diversity and Change

Since the nineteenth century, the United States had been a mixture of many faiths, with Protestantism as the dominant religion. By 1980, Protestants were still dominant, but were declining as a percent of the population. Their numbers had dropped from about 70 percent in 1960 to 65 percent. Judaism declined from 5 percent of American adults to about 3 percent. But Catholics, over the same period, rose from 28 percent of the adult population to 35 percent in 1980. This was partly due to immigration.

In these decades, a lively interest in ethnic culture developed. The term "multicultural" was coined to describe a nation composed of many peoples, each with unique characteristics. Celebrating "multiculturalism" means different cultures are respected and accepted. Multiculturalism includes traditions in music, dress, and food, and especially in worship—the heart of most cultures. America had been shaped by "cultural pluralism," which is many different cultures living close together. Now, there was "religious pluralism" as never before.

In this time of change, many Americans followed unusual paths to find answers to questions of belief. Some attempted to explore their consciousness and spirituality by using illegal "mind-altering" drugs. Other seekers developed their own systems of belief. Many followed charismatic leaders, strong individuals whose personalities appealed to their followers. Still others began to study nature worship, tribal religions, the occult, and they tried meditation and yoga.

By the late 1970s, numerous Native Americans were rediscovering their own original faiths. In the larger population there was also broad interest in Native culture. This impulse was inspired by the study of American Indian spirituality and philosophy. As the environmental movement grew, Americans gained new understanding of ecology by observing Native American respect for nature. In the late 1800s, the government had suppressed native religious practices. There even was a law against Native Americans practicing their ancient rituals. That ban officially came to an end in 1978, when the American Indian Religious Freedom Act was passed by Congress.

In part, the act read: "Henceforth it shall be the policy of the United States to protect and preserve for American Indians their inherent right of freedom to believe, express and exercise the traditional religions [including] . . . access to sites, use and possession of sacred objects, and the freedom to worship through ceremonials and traditional rites."

Faith Strengthens Activists

The Civil Rights movement of the 1960s was inspired by religion. The moral foundations of faith gave strength to those struggling for African American rights.

African American Baptist denominations and their young ministers led the Civil Rights movement. The most notable ministers were Martin Luther King, Jr., Ralph Abernathy, Andrew Young, and Jessie Jackson. King might have been speaking for all ministers in the movement when he said, "Religion has been real to me and closely knitted to life. In fact the two cannot be separated; religion for me is life."

King was also inspired by the pacifist teachings of India's Mahatma Gandhi. Using the power of nonviolent resistance, Gandhi had led his own people to freedom in the 1940s. African Americans and their allies won admiration around the world for courageously practicing nonviolent resistance against unjust laws and their oppressive enforcers.

Like King, Malcolm Little was the son of a Baptist preacher. But while King went to college, Little went to prison, for

Dr. Martin Luther King, Jr. was a Baptist minister.
(Library of Congress)

armed robbery. There, he converted to an American Muslim group, and changed his name to Malcolm X. Emerging a free man, he became minister to the African American Nation of Islam, where he rejected nonviolence as the only path to civil rights. "By any means necessary," became his slogan. Frustrated by the slow pace of nonviolence, many African Americans looked to Malcolm X for leadership.

Unlike African American churches, few predominantly white religious bodies took a formal stand in favor of civil rights. Yet, many individual clergy and lay people were active in the movement. Especially in its early years, Jews and white Christians marched in solidarity with African Americans.

In these years, Americans of all faiths also tried to do something about illiteracy and poverty. They carried on the "social gospel" traditions of the early twentieth century. This movement tried to improve society through education and political reform. Many volunteered to help in charitable organizations, such as orphanages and homes for troubled children. Some taught the poor to read. Others helped to register black voters, risking attacks by white racists. Congregations from all over America donated millions of dollars to help the needy.

Conflict in the House of Worship

Religious leaders and congregations experienced new difficulties in this time of social change. The most deeply felt religious conflicts were no longer between one religion and another. Instead, conflicts were more to be found within each religion. This was largely because of members taking sides on political questions. Nearly every religious group had inner differences over issues such as abortion rights, the Vietnam War, and women's rights. Most had "liberal" and "conservative" wings. Fundamentalist Christians came to share many opinions with conservative Catholics, especially with regard to abortion and women's issues.

One of the major issues that caused discord was whether women could be ordained as clergy. The Catholic Church forbade it and Baptists opposed it as well. However, some Protestant denominations began to ordain women by the 1960s. The controversy was especially strong in the Episcopal Church, which also ordained women. Opposition resulted in some Episcopal congregations splitting off from the main church. Reform Judaism—a branch of the Jewish faith—also ordained several women as rabbis. The two other main branches, Conservative and Orthodox, did not.

Polls in the late 1960s indicated that half the country believed religious life was declining. About 78 percent of Americans believed morals were failing, and 75 percent believed religion's influence was diminishing. In this period, the percent of adults who regularly attended religious services went down. Protestant attendance dropped from about 43 to 36 percent. Catholic attendance declined from 72 percent to 50 percent.

Jews Look to Traditions of Faith

The many thousands of Jewish refugees who came from Europe after World War II were a diverse people. They ranged from sophisticated Austrian moderns to peasants from the Polish farmlands. By 1960, America's approximately six million Jews were the world's largest and most influential Jewish population. Each of the religion's three main groups—Orthodox,

A young man in Seattle, Washington stands with his father, grandfather, and rabbi just before his bar mitzvah, in 1970. (CORBIS)

Conservative, and Reform—had its own rabbis and synagogues. All three forms of observance originally developed in the 1800s.

Orthodox Judaism follows traditions handed down over the centuries. This includes praying in Hebrew, the ancient language of the Jewish people. Most Jewish immigrants from Eastern Europe were Orthodox.

Like Orthodox Judaism, Conservative Judaism stresses the ancient traditions of worship and culture. Saturday is the Jewish Sabbath, they only eat Kosher food (food specially approved by a rabbi), and they pray in Hebrew. Conservatives see Judaism as more than a religious practice. To them, Judaism is an expression of a nation and its historical culture. Conservative Jews often look to the Hebrew culture of ancient times to find guidance for their daily lives and faith.

Reform Jews believe in assimilating with mainstream society in the country where they live. This branch of Judaism was brought to America with German-Jewish immigrants. It rejects the "separatist" practices of Orthodox Conservative Judiasm, such as head coverings for men and eating only Kosher food. Reform Jews pray mostly in English, and their synagogues have adopted customs similar to Christianity. This includes holding services on Sunday and organizing choirs.

Although many American Jews do not formally practice Judaism, their heritage is essential to them. In this period there was a surge of interest in exploring their religion's cultural and spiritual roots. Schools to study Hebrew and Jewish culture sprang up across the nation. Nearly two-thirds of America's one million Jewish children took up the study of Judaism and its culture and traditions.

Roman Catholics Enter a New Era

Early in the 1960s, all the world's Catholic bishops—leaders of national churches—were invited to take part in the Second Vatican Council in Rome. The council revised traditional doctrines to make them more acceptable to the modern worshipper. For example, the Church had always celebrated mass in Latin, the ancient language of Rome. Now the council approved saying mass in the local language of the parishioners. Also, the council ended the tradition of not eating meat on Fridays.

While the Catholic Church did not approve of divorce, after

A priest at New Ulm Cathedral in New Ulm, Minnesota offers a worshipper communion in 1974. (National Archives)

Vatican II, it made a process called annulment easier to obtain, as long as the couple had not had any children. Although divorced persons were forbidden from remarrying in the Catholic Church, those who had had previous marriages annuled were allowed to remarry in a Catholic ceremony.

One major source of controversy remained in effect: the church's opposition to birth control by using contraception. Not only did many American Catholics object, but so did those who believed the world was threatened by overpopulation.

Perhaps the most important change that came out of Vatican II was Catholicism's position toward other religions. Until now, the church had warned members not to associate too freely with non-Catholics. Now, the bishops called upon Catholics to "build bridges" with other faiths. Catholics were to cooperate for common ecumenical goals. Ecumenical generally means the coming-together of different faiths to communicate and cooperate. After Vatican II, the church was against prejudice of all kinds, whether religious or racial. The church formally opposed anti-Semitism, or prejudice against Jews.

The council gave local parishes more control over their affairs. One reason for this was the steady decline in the number of priests. Fewer priests were available to administer the day-to-day business of churches. Lay members of the congregation were increasingly needed for administration. They also aided the priest in the mass. Yet, the church opposed women becoming priests, stating that it was not the woman's spiritual task.

Three times in this period, Roman Catholics experienced the jolt of losing the pope, their spiritual leader. In 1963, Pope John XXIII died and was succeeded by Pope Paul VI, who served from 1963 until his death in 1978. John Paul I, who died very soon after taking office, succeeded Paul. He was followed by Polish-born John Paul II, who delighted American Catholics by visiting their country in 1979.

John Paul's appearance especially thrilled the large Polish-American population that had immigrated to the United States after World War II. He made a pilgrimage to a number of cities, addressing vast crowds of the faithful. John Paul spoke of the need to defend human rights and champion the world's poor. The new pope remained opposed to contraception, abortion, and women priests.

The more open attitude of the Catholic Church after Vatican II greatly influenced other religions. For one thing, they were inspired to hold interfaith conferences to discuss how religions could better cooperate.

Changes in Protestant Churches

Protestant churches also changed some of their own teachings. Sunday school texts, for example, were examined for religious prejudice.

The National Council of Churches (NCC) worked with many ecumenical and interfaith organizations. Established in 1950 as an association of Protestant denominations, the NCC now represented tens of millions of people. These included Protestant churches of British, German, and Scandinavian origin, African American churches, and immigrant churches from Korea and India. Also participating were Greek Orthodox churches with religious and cultural roots in Greece, Syria, Russia, the Ukraine, Egypt, and India. Known as a liberal organization, the NCC reached out to many other faiths and cultivated harmonious relations.

During this era, the Baptists were the largest Protestant denomination, and in these decades their numbers rose steadily. In 1960, Baptists were approximately 37 percent of all Protestants. In 1980, they accounted for about 41 percent. Methodists declined from 18 percent of Protestants in 1960 to less than 15 percent in 1980. Other denominations won more converts. Evangelical, Pentecostal, and fundamentalist churches grew in membership and strength.

In general, evangelical Christians consider Jesus to be their "personal savior." An evangelist is one who preaches the Gospel, the "good news," as certain teachings of the New Testament are termed. Pentecostals believe they are practicing the original faith of Christianity's first days. The born-again movement was another mighty religious movement in this time. It describes those who believe they have experienced a spiritual rebirth through the power of Jesus Christ. This inspiration affected members of many faiths. By 1978, 40 percent of Americans considered themselves to be "born again" because of a religious experience.

Fundamentalists consider the Bible to be perfect, without error, and they accept its texts literally. Most members of these faiths are inspired to spread the Gospel, as they have experienced it, to all others in their lives. Evangelicals, fundamentalists, and Pentecostals usually oppose liberal notions of child rearing and education. They also disagree with teaching the biological Theory of Evolution in public schools.

The Theory of Evolution maintains that all life, including human life, evolved from simpler life forms. Fundamentalists countered with Creationist Theory. This theory asserts that humans were created by God in one instant. Christian Creationists quote the Bible as proof of their belief.

Both conservative Protestant and Catholic Christians are united in their opposition to abortion. Millions of them united to create a "pro-life" political movement. They sometimes called themselves the Moral Majority, and solidly supported the conservative branch of the Republican Party. They became organized nationally thanks in part to "Televangelism," church services broadcast on nation-wide television.

Nontraditional Spirituality

Mainstream religion often labels small spiritual groups as "cults." This term generally describes a group that has one strong leader who demands strict loyalty. Members usually must change their lives drastically. They often leave families, friends, and jobs to follow the cult leader. Cults are accused of using mind-control techniques and destroying their followers' free will. Members are often young and impressionable and lonely.

By the 1970s, one of the fastest-growing nontraditional

Television Boosts Evangelism

Each week, in the comfort of their living rooms, Americans watched religious services on television. Religious broadcasting, or "televangelism" became immensely popular during the 1960s and 1970s. Some preachers had churches of their own. Others regarded television viewers as their congregants. Many viewers donated to the organizations led by televangelists, who became extremely wealthy.

One of the first and most successful "televangelist" was Oral Roberts. Roberts had one of the most popular religious programs on television. It was broadcast across the nation and watched by millions. Roberts practiced "faith healing," by which he claimed to cure audience members who had enough faith. Also popular were Pentacostal Jimmy Swaggart in Louisiana and Robert Schuller, a Dutch Reform minister in California who was more liberal.

The public appetite for such programming seemed endless. Other evangelical preachers created their own "television ministries" and rose to national fame. Their organizations became immensely profitable. American religion also included drive-in churches. There, the congregation sat in their cars for the service, as in a drive-in movie theater.

Evangelists usually preached to people of many different denominations. Nationally known minister Billy Graham, for example, preached a "Christian Gospel" message that was essentially Protestant. Yet, its broad appeal attracted millions from many denominations who were inspired by his ministry. Graham preached in major venues such as Madison Square Garden in New York. The services he led were also broadcast on television. Throughout this era, Graham was the nation's leading evangelist preacher.

organizations was the Unification Church of minister Sun Myung Moon. Known as "Moonies," the members gave complete loyalty to Moon, a native of South Korea. Group loyalty required members to marry whomever Moon chose for them. He was famous for holding mass wedding ceremonies where he married thousands of people at the same time.

Most small spiritual groups rejected being placed in the category of a cult. Their members considered themselves serious seekers of meaningful spirituality. Many had turned away from the conventional routine of organized religion. Often, they created their own structures, subjects, and ways of worship. Jesus Freaks, for example, lived counterculture lifestyles that fit into their spiritual belief. One aspect of this movement was communal living in "families," where everything was shared equally. These believers were passionate evangelists. In the 1970s, numerous Christian coffeehouses appeared, featuring contemporary folk music and a religious message. More than one such coffeehouse was called "His Place," meaning it was dedicated to Christ.

Other seekers practiced various forms of yoga and meditation. By the late 1960s, interest in India's Hindu spirituality was widespread. Pop stars, such as the Beatles, embraced Transcendental Meditation. This was a worldwide organization led by an Indian yogi (one who practices yoga). Many other yogis found followings in America, as did teachers of Buddhism. Meditation centers opened in communities across the nation, growing and prospering. In 1979, the U.S. Court of Appeals recognized Transcendental Meditation as a religion.

Religion, the Constitution, and the Courts

One of the most hotly debated subjects during this time was the relationship between religion and government. This is generally known as "church and state." The issue of keeping religion and government separate hinges on a clause in the First Amendment to the Constitution, which states: "Congress shall make no law respecting an establishment of religion, or prohibiting the free exercise thereof."

This so-called Establishment Clause has been interpreted to mean that Congress cannot officially establish or favor any religion over another. Some say government may not promote religious practices in public institutions, such as schools. Others disagree.

Debate over this amendment brought about a number of U.S. Supreme Court cases in the 1960s and 1970s.

A 1961 ruling said applicants for public office were not required to swear they believed in the existence of a god. It called such requirements a "religious test," which violated the Establishment Clause.

In 1962, the Supreme Court forbade religious ceremonies in public schools. In this landmark case, *Engel v. Vitale*, the court found that prayer and Bible-reading in schools were unconstitutional. Since the public school system is considered part of the government, schools were ordered not to sponsor prayer or devotional readings.

Two important public school cases were decided in 1963. In one, Bible-reading over the school intercom was ruled unconstitutional. The court also declared it unconstitutional to force a school child to participate in Bible-reading and prayer.

Then the leadership of the public school system of New York State composed a special prayer for schools. The Supreme Court considered this prayer to be a "religious activity." It ruled that government-sponsored school prayers put pressure on children from religious minorities to conform to "officially approved religion." They were not allowed.

A 1968 case involved the opposing theories of evolution and creationism. The court said a state cannot alter school courses in order to promote a religious point of view. Specifically, it said that any law banning the teaching of evolution would be unconstitutional. In 1980, the court judged the posting of the Ten Commandments in schools to be unconstitutional.

Taken together, these decisions provoked outrage among conservative Protestants. Many would take their children out of public schools and teach them at home or send them to newly formed religious schools. They gave momentum to the movement that would become known as the Christian Right.

Tolerance Prevails

By the end of this era, religious prejudice was less socially acceptable than it once had been. Respect for other religions became normal as people of all walks of life mingled in suburbs, schools, colleges, and in the military. Diverse faiths were becoming a distinct part of America's new multicultural character.

An indication of lessening religious prejudice can be seen in a poll from the time. It asked whether a person would vote for a "well qualified" Jew or Catholic for president. In 1960, about 72 percent of Americans said they would vote for a Jew, and 74 percent for a Catholic. By 1980, those percentages were approximately 84 for a Jew and 91 for a Catholic.

Religion was still important in the United States, but it wore many faces.

Chapter Seven

Health, Science, and Technology

Many scientific and technological advances of the 1960s and 1970s were driven by research and development for military and space programs. Communications and weather satellites soon orbited the earth. So did American astronauts and Soviet cosmonauts. In military technology, nuclear bombs could destroy the world many times. Still, it was the peaceful use of nuclear power that was needed most.

These decades saw momentous advances, such as men landing on the moon, far-reaching new anti-pollution regulations, and ultrasound medical diagnostic machines. American daily life was also improved by more common inventions. This was the same era that supermarket price scanners using "bar codes" were introduced. Also, the first auto-focus camera went on sale for the first time.

Soon to touch every aspect of the daily lives of most members of the American public was the swiftly developing field of computers. The close of the 1970s saw an explosion in computer technology. It was a revolution in achievement and invention not seen since the industrial progress of the late nineteenth century.

A doctor (LEFT) **examines a set of X-rays.** (National Library of Medicine) **In 1965, Astronaut Edward White** (RIGHT) **becomes the first American to walk in space.** (National Aeronautics and Space Administration)

Space Exploration

The space race between the United States and the Soviet Union found the Soviets in the lead as the 1960s began. In 1961, they put the first human being into orbit around the earth. Cosmonaut Yuri Gagarin's flight amazed the world and gave the Soviets bragging rights. At the same time, the United States National Aeronautical and Space Administration (NASA) had its own achievements. NASA launched *Tiros I*, the world's first weather satellite, for forecasting and research. NASA also launched *Echo I*, the first communications satellite. This pioneer satellite led the way for a new, worldwide communications system.

In 1961, NASA sent its own first astronaut into space. Navy commander Alan B. Shepard was aboard the *Freedom 7* for a flight of 15 minutes from Cape Canaveral to an Atlantic splashdown, 302 miles away. Shepard flew at an altitude of 116 miles. He was followed in 1963 by John H. Glenn, the first American to orbit the earth. Glenn's space capsule went three times around the earth in a flight of four hours and 55 minutes.

In the less glamorous, but extremely important development of communications satellites, *Telstar* went into orbit in 1962. Telstar created a worldwide communications network for telephone, television broadcasts, and data transmission.

The United States space program offered the nation many exciting moments, a number of them watched live on television. Various missions were familiar household names: Pioneer, Gemini, Jupiter, and Apollo. The world watched as the Soviets and Americans took turns making "soft," unmanned landings on the moon and on Venus. The Americans achieved the first docking of two vehicles in space and took the lead in preparing for a manned flight to the moon.

Profound tragedy struck NASA's efforts in 1967. As the *Apollo* capsule was about to launch, a fire broke out. The blaze killed the three astronauts on board. Despite this disaster, NASA pushed on and achieved the greatest triumph of all the space race. In 1969, America landed the first men on the moon. Neil Armstrong and Buzz Aldrin touched down, in *Apollo 11*, on July 20. As he stepped from the space capsule, Armstrong said, "That's one small step for man, one giant leap for mankind." The astronauts sent back live photographs from the moon. Among these images was "Earth Rising," an image of the green and blue planet from

Astronaut Buzz Aldrin prepares to become the second man to walk on the moon. The first, Neil Armstrong, took this photograph. (National Aeronautics and Space Administration)

the moon, which remained popular for decades to come.

In 1972, the government authorized a $5.5 billion program to build a "space shuttle." The shuttle was designed to orbit the earth as a spaceship and land as a glider. The aircraft was expected to be ready in six years.

In the mid-1970s, space technology progressed steadily. Skylab, the first American space station, was launched in 1973. More manned trips were made to the moon. The last, *Apollo 17*, brought back samples of rock and soil for study. Unmanned space probes were launched to further explore the moon as well as Jupiter, Mars, Saturn, Uranus, and Venus. In 1974, the first international space project took place. *Apollo 18* and the Soviets' *Soyuz 19* linked up in space to conduct joint experiments.

Through these years, the development of the space shuttle continued. The program was billions of dollars above budget and three years behind schedule when the space shuttle *Columbia* first flew in 1979. *Columbia* was a triumph of engineering, and its flight was a proud moment nationally. It was the first time in five years that the United States had sent humans into space.

Pesticide Pollution

By the mid-1960s, concern was rising that the use of the pesticide DDT had serious disadvantages. After World War II, DDT had proven highly effective in controlling mosquitoes and many insects that attack food crops. Research showed, however, there were major problems. For one, insects developed an immunity to the pesticide. Also, birds and fish that ate insects exposed to DDT began to die as a result. DDT in small quantities was judged nontoxic to humans, but it could accumulate in the body over a period of time.

Widely used in agriculture since the 1940s, DDT also created new imbalances in insect groups. While one group was eliminated, others appeared and took their place. The balance of nature was being tipped by the overuse of artificial pesticides. In this time, Americans were becoming much more concerned about the environment and how it affected their health. The 1962 best-selling book, *Silent Spring*, by Rachel Carson, discussed the danger of insecticides to birds and beneficial insects. Carson is credited for stimulating the founding of the environmental movement. As an indication of public thinking regarding the environment, the first Earth Day was celebrated in the spring of 1970. This event would eventually become an enormous festival around the world, in the spirit of promoting a healthy environment.

Rachel Carson
(Library of Congress)

In 1972, government regulations sharply controlled the use of DDT. This pesticide never regained its place as the preferred, toxic solution for controlling insects.

The growing public demand to fight pollution was met by Congress's passage of both the Clean Water Act and the Clean Air Act in 1970. This landmark legislation came during President Nixon's first term in office. Nixon signed the bills despite resistance from entrenched business and political opposition. They feared that the new regulations would bring new costs and loss of profits. These acts had far-reaching results that notably improved the environment. For example, the Clean Air Act required automakers to build engines that would be 90 percent emission-free. It also placed strict limits on air pollution from power plants, among the worst polluters in the country.

Nuclear Power

New military uses for nuclear power were demonstrated in 1962 when the first nuclear warhead was test-fired from the nuclear-powered submarine, USS *Polaris*. Despite the thousands of nuclear weapons ready for action, peaceful nuclear power applications were also on the drawing board. One pioneering use was the first nuclear-powered lighthouse, built in Chesapeake Bay in 1964. Through the 1960s, nuclear power was seen as the nation's best future energy source.

There was a growing need for more power in these years. The power industry began to have serious difficulty meeting new demand. Previously, electricity use had grown at seven or eight percent each year. Now, sudden growth in population and industry in certain regions required additional generating capacity. For example, the Virginia Electric Power Company had several 14 percent growth years.

In some places during hot summer days, power companies feared that high electrical demand would cause power outages and equipment damage. Several companies were forced to temporarily reduce voltage to parts of their network of customers. These were termed "brownouts," meaning power was not shut off, but full power was not available for a while. In November 1965, a "blackout" left seven states from Maine to New York in the dark for a day. The same thing happened again in July 1977, but by then equipment made it possible to confine the blackout to a single place—New York City.

A number of problems faced the power companies. For one, there was a shortage of fuel to run the plants. Coal was less available because many mines were closing down. Mine operators expected nuclear power to become the only fuel for new generating plants. At the same time, oil was becoming more expensive. The federal Clean Air Act of 1970 placed new limitations on air pollution. Oil pumped in the United States often had high sulfur content, which polluted too much. Therefore, power companies turned to foreign suppliers, especially in the Middle East, whose oil burned cleaner. After political and military conflicts in the Middle East in 1973, the price of oil shot up from $2 per barrel to more than $12.

Industry expectations for nuclear power began to wane by the early 1970s. Nuclear technology was proving to have its own problems. For one thing, nuclear-fired power plants caused "thermal pollution" of rivers and waterways. Water was taken into the plant to cool equipment. When it was sent back to the river, its higher temperature killed fish and affected aquatic life. It became increasingly expensive for utilities to obey regulations against thermal pollution. In addition to these higher operating costs, nuclear-fired plants were more expensive to build. New plants were required to meet ever-changing pollution and safety regulations. Building a nuclear-fired plant cost five times the price of a conventional plant. Further, nuclear plants were more complex, so they took much longer to build. Coal-burning plants needed eight years to construct, while nuclear plants needed 12 years.

Even worse, the safety systems of nuclear-fired power plants were too often inadequate. Leaks of radioactive materials were dangerous to anyone exposed to them. In 1972, the Atomic Energy Commission, which governed nuclear power, admitted that nuclear plants were not as safe as they should be. Accidents at nuclear plants in the mid-1970s indicated that nuclear power could be dangerous in the long run. The nuclear power industry suffered a major blow in March 1979. A radioactive leak at

Three Mile Island
(National Archives)

Three Mile Island nuclear power plant in Pennsylvania terrified the nation. The reactor threatened to melt down. A national television audience watched anxiously as 144,000 residents of the region were evacuated.

The emergency passed without disaster. However, much of the population now doubted that nuclear-fired power generation would meet America's ever-growing energy needs.

Health and Medicine

Medical advances of this period included the first heart-bypass surgery and the first heart transplant operation. In 1963, medicine saw the use of an artificial heart in an operation. The first human heart was transplanted on a patient in South Africa in 1967. It was followed a year later by the first implantation of an artificial heart. These early patients did not live very long, but the operations laid the groundwork for future procedures.

In 1982 University of Utah surgeons successfully transplanted a human heart with an artificial heart. Transplants of various biological organs, including kidneys and livers, would be common by the close of this era.

Electronic medical diagnoses advanced in 1972 with the introduction of the CAT scan—Computerized Axial Tomography. The CAT scan uses X-rays to show a cross-section view of the patient's interior, thus reducing the need for invasive, "exploratory" surgery. CAT scans made it easier for physicians to diagnose illnesses or internal injuries.

Other medical science developments included the improved use of ultrasound for diagnostics. Ultrasound employs high frequency sound waves to create images of the interior of the body. Because the vibration is mechanical, ultrasound is safer than diagnostic tests that use radiation. It is best known for showing the development of a fetus. Also, in 1978, the first test-tube baby was born, in England. The baby was created by artificially inseminating a woman's egg and then implanting the egg in the mother's womb. There, the baby grows normally, as if the egg had been fertilized in the mother's body.

In 1977, the first "balloon anigoplasty" was performed in San Francisco to treat coronary artery disease. This procedure involves opening collapsed arteries by inserting tiny "balloons" that can be inflated to clear the blockage.

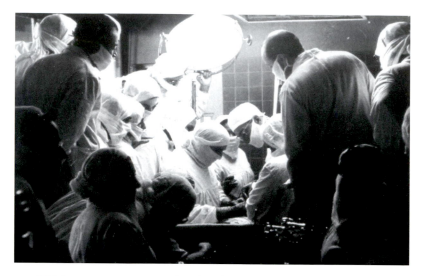

A group of doctors observe a heart surgeon at work. (National Library of Medicine)

With many new medical advances, the modern hospital achieved marvels in patient care and diagnosis. At the same time, hospitals were too often unsuccessful financially. Many small, local hospitals teetered on the edge of bankruptcy. They began to transform themselves from not-for-profit status into for-profit businesses. This usually promised higher medical costs in the future.

The care of the mentally ill saw drastic changes in how society treated these patients. In the 1960s, only half the needed beds were available for patients who needed treatment. Until then, efforts to care for them had been conducted mainly at the state and local levels. Now, federal funds were made available to create local centers to treat the mentally ill. These patients were expected to be happier living in residences rather than in large mental institutions. Although the theory was well-meaning, the programs were under-funded, and the policy often contributed to wandering and homelessness for many individuals.

Warnings against Smoking

During the early 1960s, Americans increasingly worried about the health hazards of smoking. In 1964, the United States Surgeon General determined for the first time that smoking posed serious health risks. Despite this and other reports about the dangers of smoking, 70 million Americans still smoked.

The federal government required warnings on cigarette packs and advertising in 1964. Over the years, the warning was changed, becoming more ominous. At first, it read: "Caution: Cigarette Smoking May Be Hazardous to Your Health." By 1970, it was more definite: "Warning: The Surgeon General Has Determined That Cigarette Smoking Is Dangerous to Your Health."

The 1967 Surgeon General's report stated that smoking was the principal cause of lung cancer. Smoking was also linked to heart disease. Two years later, in 1969, Pan American Airlines created the first non-smoking section. In 1970, TWA became the first airline to offer no-smoking sections aboard every aircraft in its fleet.

By 1970, tobacco was the most heavily advertised product in America. In this year, Congress banned cigarette advertising on radio and television. This was in part to prevent advertising from persuading young people to take up smoking. The law cost the broadcast industry about $220 million in lost tobacco advertising revenue.

A major anti-smoking milepost came with the Surgeon General's report of 1972. It found there was a danger to non-smokers who were exposed to tobacco smoke, termed "second-hand smoke." Six out of ten Americans now believed that smoking was hazardous to the non-smoker's health. Tobacco industry leaders considered this controversy to be "the most dangerous development yet to the viability of the tobacco industry." This would prove true in decades to come, as non-smokers' rights forced new anti-smoking regulations.

The federal government required all airlines to have non-smoking sections in 1973. In this year, Arizona passed a law restricting smoking in public places. Other states began to follow Arizona's lead. Spontaneous anti-smoking movements grew up. Spurred on by high-school students, communities across the nation chose to go "non-smoking" for a day. Each year, these scattered events increased in number. Then, in 1977, the effort went national as the first "Great American Smoke-out."

In 1979, insurance company research stated, "Cigarette smokers are subject to a mortality risk significantly higher than that of non-smokers." Since insurance policies are based on the health and lifestyle of the insured client, smokers were a higher insurance risk than non-smokers. The result was that insurance companies charged smokers higher premiums for health insurance policies.

The wealthy and politically powerful tobacco industry continued to oppose anti-smoking legislation and negative public health reports. Regarding the health dangers of smoking, the industry's lawyers argued that the case was not proved. Yet, even stricter limits would be placed on smoking in public places, such as restaurants and schools. The tobacco industry had been right to fear that controversy over second-hand smoke would become the most potent anti-tobacco issue of the future.

Flight, Lasers, and Media

For all the improvements in airplane design in this time, one of the most popular innovations came in 1964 with the first in-flight movies. Movies were welcome on long flights that were becoming increasingly common. By 1968, "jumbo jets" had revolutionized commercial flight, doubling passenger capacity and increasing flight range to 6,000 miles.

A few years later, in 1976, Air France and British Airways begin the first regularly scheduled commercial supersonic transport (SST) flights. Known as the Concorde, these supersonic passenger jets were best known on the New York-Paris transatlantic route.

The world's first working laser was built in the United States in 1960. Lasers would find many important uses in manufacturing and technology in the next two decades. The narrow light beam produced by lasers maintains its size and direction over very large distances. It can be sharply focused to cut and bore metals and other materials. In medicine, lasers are used in surgical operations. Lasers are also used in scientific research, in communications equipment, and in military weapons.

Communications developments were stimulated by the advance of technology in the 1960s and 1970s. Television dominated broadcast communication more than ever. By the mid-1960s there were more than 600 commercial television stations in the United States, compared with 29 in 1948. More than 10 million televisions were being manufactured annually. The first transatlantic television transmission took place in 1962. This transmission used the recently launched Telstar communications satellite, which made worldwide television and cable broadcast possible.

Although television was the favorite medium, radio made an unexpected comeback in popularity. For one thing, radios were in every automobile. That meant millions of listeners, commuting every day, were the potential audience. At first, AM radio was the only band available in cars. Then, in the 1970s, FM radio soared in popularity. Traveling over shorter distances, FM produced bet-

The Environmentalist President

When President Carter came to office in 1977, one of his prime objectives was for America to achieve energy "independence." Carter saw conservation of energy as the key to energy independence. He faced powerful political and business opposition to changing how things were done. Oil companies wanted to continue making high profits. Most automobile manufacturers did not want to make smaller, more fuel-efficient cars. Despite the opposition, Carter set out to stimulate the development of alternative power sources, such as solar power.

Carter made a television broadcast to the nation, announcing his plan. He called the energy crisis of the late 1970s the "moral equivalent of war." He said Americans were the world's greatest wasters of energy. It was essential, he said, to promote energy-saving appliances and industrial equipment. He described energy conservation as the "most practical source of energy."

To encourage conservation, Carter called for tax credits for the insulation of homes, stores, and factories. He also sought greater production of coal and oil and further use of nuclear power plants. At the same time, he promoted the development of other energy resources. Carter pushed for federal funding of alternative energy devices, including solar cells, geothermal energy, and wind turbines. In this way, with conservation and new technologies, America could move away from dependence on foreign oil.

Carter had solar collectors installed on the White House, and new technologies were inspired by his leadership. The first geothermal generator was developed in 1978. This generator uses the warmer temperatures of the earth's interior to collect energy. The principle involves extracting heat through pipes driven deep into the earth. Other geothermal energy methods tap natural hot springs far below the ground and capture the steam power they produce.

These and other novel concepts had a considerable following at the time. Companies and individuals, both, began to work on alternative energy sources. There was hope the federal government would enthusiastically back the research. At the end of Carter's term in 1980, however, most federal programs for alternative energy were abruptly dropped. President Reagan even removed the solar collectors from the White House.

ter sound and FM stations played a wider variety of music than AM stations.

In 1963, the first push-button phones were marketed. Push button dialing would not replace the rotary dial until the 1980s. By then, computer technology and electronics were opening the door to communications that once seemed only science fiction.

Computers

By the start of the 1960s, the number of computers in the United States had grown to 17,000 (up from just 15 computers in 1954). These computers served the military and scientific and scholarly researchers. Their main function had been for calculations in complex mathematical functions. In 1960, the Common Business Oriented Language (COBOL) was developed by computer manufacturers in collaboration with the Pentagon.

Most computer developments of the 1960s had little direct effect on daily life. Yet, computer studies were slowly gaining a following in higher education. In 1964 Dartmouth College professors created BASIC, an easy-to-learn programming language, for their students. Technical advances in hardware and software progressed steadily. Computer technology was in the limelight in 1968, when the Apollo Guidance Computer orbited the Earth on *Apollo 7*.

In 1970, International Business Machines (IBM) dominated the business and institutional market with its "mainframe computers." But computers were room-size. People accessed them through "work stations" at their desks, but they all shared the same processor.

A technician adjusts a mainframe computer. (©Ed Eckstein/CORBIS)

In 1971, Intel introduced the microprocessor, the "computer on a chip." This tiny integrated circuit, or microchip, was the basis of the computer revolution that followed. It made it possible to make computers much, much smaller.

Everyday computer use came closer in 1971, when Texas Instruments released the first pocket calculator. The Pocketronic, could add, subtract, multiply, and divide. It weighed about 2.5 pounds and cost $150. New word-processing systems appeared. Word processors began to replace office typewriters. In 1975 the Altair "home computer kit" made it possible for individuals to build and program their own personal computers.

In 1977, Steve Jobs and Stephen Wozniak launched their Apple II. This smaller "personal" computer was an instant success in the home market. The Apple II came with 4 kilobytes of RAM, game paddles, and a cassette tape with the computer game "Breakout." The first personal computer with color graphics, but it came without a monitor. Users had to hook the machine to their televisions. Nevertheless, the Apple II sold for $1,300. The Apple had two competitors, Tandy Radio Shack's TRS-80 and the Commodore PET. Both cost about half as much as the Apple. Tandy, sold 10,000 units in its initial month. (The company had projected sales of 3,000 units for its first full year.) But the Apple II proved to be more lasting, partly because it had extra slots to add more memory and other devices.

Also in 1977, Microsoft, founded by Bill Gates and Paul Allen, began to take off as a software company. Gates and Allen created the first computer language programs for personal computers.

In 1980, Apple Computer tried to enter the business market with the Apple III. It had 128 KB RAM, and, depending on its configuration, cost from $4,500 to $8,000. But the model was a technical failure. Apple fell back on its Apple II sales, which reached $140 million over three years. IBM would not introduce a personal computer until 1981. When it did, the two companies would face off.

By the end of the 1970s, more than one million computers were already in use in the United States.

Chapter Eight

Leisure, Sports, and Entertainment

The cast of *M.A.S.H.*, (LEFT) **one of television's most popular programs during the 1970s.** (Movie Star News) **Joan Baez and Bob Dylan** (RIGHT) (National Archives)

The generation that came of age at the beginning of the 1960s had more time and money for leisure and entertainment than any previous generation. "Baby boomers," as this generation was called, had weekly allowances, and many worked part-time. They could afford to go to the movies, attend ball games, buy cars, and travel. They also bought records and attended music performances as never before. The entertainment industry blossomed to meet their interests.

Television was mainly about entertainment, from music to sports to comedies. However, television was not the only source of entertainment. During the 1960s and 1970s, more people than ever went to the movies. More people purchased books. In addition, participation sports boomed. Outdoor activities such as running, biking, or hiking also became popular.

By the end of the Seventies, spectator sports were a main product of network television. Pro athletes were celebrities, part of the world of entertainment. One of the biggest box-office movie hits of the era tapped the nation's love of sport and its sympathy for the underdog: *Rocky*, the story of a boxer who fought his way to success, against the odds.

Television

During the 1960s and 1970s, television's "prime time" fare featured game shows, spy thrillers, and situation comedies. "Sitcoms," as they were termed, were often about family life. They had new episodes every week, with the same characters and a guest star or two. *The Andy Griffith Show*, about a small town sheriff, was one of the most popular. Another was *The Beverly Hillbillies*, a comedy about country folk who struck oil and moved to sophisticated Beverly Hills. The genre of science fiction and the supernatural came to television with the *Twilight Zone*, a weekly drama. Even more sci-fi was the futuristic *Star Trek*, the adventures of the crew of a military space ship in the distant future. *Batman* stepped out of the comic books for another weekly drama.

In 1972, Home Box Office (HBO) made its debut as a cable television network. HBO was the first potential competition for the national broadcasting networks. The publicly funded Corporation for Public Broadcasting won its own viewers with its children's programming, especially *Sesame Street*. Public Broadcasting was also successful with live broadcasts of important political events and hearings.

In this time, network television became more willing to air topics once forbidden. The variety shows *Rowan and Martin's Laugh-In*, *The Smothers Brothers*, and *Saturday Night Live* made fun of topics once thought of as off limits, such as sex and religion. One of the most controversial situation comedies was *All in the Family*. This sitcom's plots touched on sensitive issues, such as abortion, homosexuality, and race relations. Another popular sitcom that discussed serious issues was *M.A.S.H.*, a comedy set in an American military hospital during the Korean War. One of the great successes of the 1970s was *Roots*, a "miniseries" based on a book by Alex Hailey about African American history.

Rock, from Presley to Punk

During the 1950s, popular music had undergone big changes. Some young white musicians had begun imitating African American rhythm and blues musicians. The best-known of these white musicians was Elvis Presley. Soon other young white rock and roll stars, including Buddy Holly and Jerry Lee Lewis were following in his footsteps. Groundbreaking African American stars, such as Chuck Berry and Little Richard, also gained huge followings with white audiences, as did the young Mexican American singer, Richie Valens.

At its start, rock and roll was music that few adults appreciated—a fact that only added to its popularity with young people. However, some adults recognized that the music's popularity made for good business. By 1960, record companies had begun to seek out singers that they could market as "teen idols." Unlike Elvis Presley, who had shocked many adults with his shaking hips and rebellious attitude, teen idols like Paul Anka and Fabian were clean-cut and well-mannered.

The era of the teen idol did not last long due to three main trends. The first came in the form of The Beatles. Arriving in the United States in 1964, John Lennon, Paul McCartney, George Harrison, and Ringo Starr soon became as popular as Elvis Presley had been before them. Unlike either Elvis or the teen idols of the early 1960s, The Beatles usually wrote their own music. From 1964 to 1970, when the group broke up, The Beatles helped to reshape music. They also opened the doors of America to a "British Invasion" of popular British groups, including the Rolling Stones, who began their career by playing African American rhythm and blues songs, before developing their own unique sound.

In addition to the impact of the "British Invasion," two other trends shaped the era's music. By the 1960s, a whole wave of African American groups and artists became popular with audiences of all races. Many of these artists recorded for a Detroit, Michigan company called Motown Records. In addition to male singers like Marvin Gaye and Smokey Robinson, Motown offered "girl groups," such as Martha and the Vandellas and The Supremes. By the late 1960s, other African American artists, including the gospel music–inspired vocalist Aretha Franklin and the extraordinary electric guitarist and bandleader Jimi Hendrix would climb to the top of the charts.

A concert poster for The Supremes
(private collection)

A third major trend of the 1960s that would shape the popular music that would come later was the arrival of "folk rock." Folk music gained new popularity in the late 1950s and in the early 1960s through singers like Joan Baez and Pete Seeger, as well as through a young songwriter named Bob Dylan. By 1965, Dylan had released several records featuring both traditional folk songs and some of his own highly poetic songs. Many of his lyrics addressed political topics like war, racism, and poverty. That year, at a folk concert in Newport, Rhode Island, he shocked his fans by appearing on stage with an electric guitar. Although many of his traditional fans were disappointed, this new sound made people think about music in a new way. New folk rock bands, such as the Byrds, soon arrived on the scene. Dylan's emphasis on lyrics even influenced The Beatles, who began to write more songs with political or social commentary.

A poster for the Woodstock festival
(Library of Congress)

One of the most spectacular musical and social events of the twentieth century was the explosive Woodstock festival in the summer of 1969. Over 300,000 young people gathered on a farm north of New York City. They came to hear the current stars of folk and rock music. Among them were Crosby, Stills, Nash and Young, The Grateful Dead, The Who, Jefferson Airplane, Jimi Hendrix, and Joan Baez. The concert, which lasted three days, became a symbol for the young generation. The concert was billed "3 Days of Peace and Music and Love." To many young people, the concert was a celebration of those values.

During the 1970s, the trends that had shaped the music of the 1960s continued. Folk rock artists, such as James Taylor, The Eagles, and Linda Rondstadt, vied for space on the top of the charts with British acts such as Led Zeppelin and David Bowie, as well as African American artists like Stevie Wonder and the Jackson Five. As the decade passed, however, much of the social commentary that had been found in much of music of the 1960s gave way to more personal lyrics.

The Eagles
(Electra-Asylum Records)

In the late 1970s, yet another new sound grew out of African American music. This music wasn't about social commentary at all—just about having fun. Called "disco" because it was played in discotheques, or dance clubs, the music soon spawned several popular movies, including the hugely successful *Saturday Night Fever*. Disco stars included Donna Summer, Gloria Gaynor, and the BeeGees.

As the 1970s closed, two more styles of music, both of which first developed in New York City, were just coming into their own. One, called "punk," had grown out of music clubs of lower Manhattan before becoming popular in England. The other, called "rap" first came out of New York's Bronx neighborhood. Punk, usually played by whites, was loud and fast, and often angry. Rap, usually performed by African Americans, featured spoken word lyrics, or a rap, over a steady beat. Although neither style attracted a large audience at the time, they both would become more popular over the next several decades.

Audrey Hepburn (Library of Congress)

All Kinds of Movies

American moviegoers began the decade of the 1960s with the shock of Marilyn Monroe's death in 1962 at age 36. This "blond bombshell" was much loved for her versatile film performances. Her onscreen personality was a blend of wit, charm, and sexiness. It saddened millions of fans to hear that Monroe had apparently taken her own life with an overdose of sleeping pills. With the death of Marilyn Monroe, Audrey Hepburn became a favorite of movie fans. Hepburn was as demure as Monroe was seductive. She was best known for such movies as *Breakfast at Tiffany's* (1961), *Charade* (1963), and *My Fair Lady* (1964).

Walt Disney's feature-length cartoons continued to be the best in "family entertainment," with *101 Dalmatians*, and *Jungle Book* being two of the most popular. Disney also produced non-animated, live-

A still from the 1970s
disaster film,
Earthquake, **starring
Charleton Heston** (LEFT)
and Ava Gardner
(RIGHT). (Movie Star News)

action movies, including *Mary Poppins* (1964) about a nanny who
could fly.

Not all the hits of this era were so light-hearted. Some reflect-
ed the on-going Cold War. *Dr. Strangelove* was a disturbing but
humorous film starring Peter Sellers as a mad scientist. Released
in 1964, *Dr. Strangelove* spoofed the nuclear arms race and the
military. James Bond was a traditional spy hero. Playing Bond,
Sean Connery had six box-office hits, including *From Russia
With Love* and *Goldfinger*. Bond movies combined sex and violence with slick settings and clever plots.

The 1960s closed with two hit films that concerned more serious themes. Dustin Hoffman was the lead in both. *The Graduate*
of 1968 portrayed the depressing confusion of a recent college
grad. *Midnight Cowboy*, in 1969, was an intimate look at a
down-and-out vagabond in New York City. In both films, the star
was not a hero, but an "antihero," a realistic person struggling
with a difficult life situation.

By the end of the 1960s, the movies were losing their audience to television. Even the once-popular drive-in movies were
going out of business. That decline reversed in the 1970s. The sci-
ence-fiction adventure, *Star Wars* (1977), was a national sensation, helping the movies to make a comeback. The special effects
developed by *Star Wars* director George Lucas were at their best
only on the big screen. The movies began to offer improved color
and Dolby sound, further outpacing television's picture and

sound. Taking advantage of improved technology, the film industry began to turn out dramatic "disaster movies." *Towering Inferno* (1974), *Earthquake* (1974), and *Poseidon Adventure* (1972) had little in the way of plot. Instead, they delivered action and spectacular imagery.

More serious 1970s films also employed powerful new film technology for dramatic and moving effects. *Apocalypse Now*, about the Vietnam War, brought the viewer starkly close to the action. So, too, did *Jaws*, the story of a killer Great White shark. This film helped launch director Steven Spielberg's career. *The Godfather*, the story of a Mafia family, had several sequels. Longtime star Marlon Brando came out of semi-retirement for this leading role. Then Sylvester Stallone wrote and starred in *Rocky*, a fighter who boxes his way to victory against all the odds. Stallone's personal triumph in making himself a film star overnight was just as remarkable as Rocky's victory in the ring.

Broadway and the Theater

This period saw many enduring musicals, including *Camelot*, *Hello Dolly*, *Fiddler on the Roof*, *Oliver*, and *Man of La Mancha*. One of the most exciting and original was *Hair*, a story of young hippies living in Manhattan in the 1960s. All were made into hit movies.

Economic times were difficult for much of this era. People could not afford to go to shows as often as in the past. At the same time, costs rose, making tickets more expensive. One result was that the audiences for theater declined. This increased the hardship for performers and theaters, especially in New York, the center of American show business. Theaters opened in other cities, where costs were lower and a fresh audience was ready and eager to attend. By 1966, for the first time, more actors were employed outside New York than in it.

The leading dramatic playwright of the era was Edward Albee, who wrote the drama *Who's Afraid of Virginia Woolf*, about a battling married couple. This play became a film, starring Elizabeth Taylor and her husband at the time, Welsh actor Richard Burton. Neil Simon kept writing one hit comedy after another. These included *Come Blow Your Horn*, (1961), *Barefoot in the Park*, (1963), *The Odd Couple* (1965) and *Promises, Promises*, (1968).

Books: A Rich Selection

American literature lost one of its leading lights in 1961 when novelist Ernest Hemingway died. A national figure and Nobel Prize winner, Hemingway had chronicled the American male experience since World War I, in which he drove an ambulance. He is said to have been suffering physical problems and mental distress when he shot himself.

The most successful novelists in these decades included Jewish writers like Philip Roth (*Goodbye Columbus*) and Joseph Heller (*Catch 22*), Southerners Walker Percy (*The Moviegoer*) and William Styron (*Sophie's Choice*), Northeasterners John Updike (*Rabbit Run* and other books about that character) and Kurt Vonnegut (*Cat's Cradle* and *Slaughterhouse Five*). African American writers James Baldwin (*The Fire Next Time*) and Toni Morrison (*The Bluest Eye* and *Song of Solomon*) also captured public attention. With the advent of the women's movement, writers like Joyce Carol Oates whose many books included *Them*, and poets Erica Jong and Marge Percy gained wide attention. James Michener whose *Tales of the South Pacific* had been turned into a popular musical continued to write novels that familiarized Americans with other parts of the world. With *The Electric Kool Aid Acid Test*, Tom Wolfe popularized nonfiction that used fictional techniques called the "new journalism." More commercial popular writers included Jacqueline Susann, Judith Krantz, and Sidney Sheldon.

The world of book publishing thrived through the 1970s. Paperbacks were the most popular purchases for readers of novels, who might buy two or three at a time. Airplane travel also stimulated book purchases. Travelers could buy a cheap paperback that would last the flight. By the end of the 1970s, however, prices rose steeply with the cost of paper and printing. More and more "paperback originals" were being published. These books were published only in paperback and would never be available in hardcover.

In 1974, a new novelist specializing in horror stories grabbed readers' attention with the publication of this first book, *Carrie*, about a high school girl possessed with horrible powers. Stephen King would go on to become one of the best-selling authors of all time. *Carrie*, as well as *The Shining*, *Christine*, and numerous other books by King, would gain even wider audiences as movies.

America at Play

Playing and competing in sports increasingly became America's favorite entertainment. Softball, volleyball, and basketball were the most played participation sports. Surfing and beach volleyball were high on the list of youth recreation, from Hawaii to New Jersey.

The rebirth of the bicycle's popularity brought a wave of new models, from racing bikes to ten-speeds. Biking was stimulated by a new widespread enthusiasm for healthy exercise. Most bicycles, which once had been considered for children, were being purchased by adults. Many Americans took up running for fitness. A boom in running shoes followed, resulting in a great variety of sneakers appearing in stores. Big-city marathons in Boston and New York developed into spectacles with tens of thousands of participants.

Tennis became more popular in the 1960s as young people took up the sport in the many newly built suburban tennis courts. Previous generations did not have access to many courts. By the end of the 1970s, almost every school and college had tennis courts. The fitness revolution brought forth many private athletic clubs. They had modern weight rooms, gymnasiums, swimming pools, spas, and courts for tennis and racketball.

Golf, too, was growing fast, with new courses constructed in the suburbs. Professional golf boomed, as colorful champions gathered enthusiastic followings. The leading personality of the late 1960s and early 1970s was Arnold Palmer. When Palmer played, he was trailed by a devoted audience of enthusiasts known as "Arnie's Army." Every weekend, television covered the Professional Golfers' Association of America tournaments. Through the mid-1970s, Palmer was was one of the top players in the game. His arch-rival was newcomer Jack Nicklaus, who eventually took over from Palmer as the world's top golfer.

Hiking, backpacking and camping became a new rage in the 1960s and 1970s. As with bikes and running shoes, new equipment appeared to meet the demand. Tents and hiking gear became lighter, easier to use, and more durable than before. Campers could drive the modern superhighways to get to distant camping areas. National and state parks were being developed for camping and picnicking. Tourism in the United States was easier than ever thanks to the new highway system. Vacations by

Hiking gained new popularity during the 1970s. This hiker, photographed in 1975, was exploring California's Sierra Mountains. (©Ted Streshinsky/CORBIS)

car, often towing a camper, were favorite leisure activities for families by the late 1960s.

Travel abroad, especially to Europe, was increasingly popular. Air travel became more common by the close of the 1960s. At the same time, travel by ship and train decreased.

Spectator sports were led by thoroughbred horse racing, baseball, and football. Stock car and formula racing were also becoming popular. Basketball was on the rise, as was soccer. Still, it was baseball that most captured the hearts of the average American.

Home Run Champs and "Amazin' Mets"

The biggest sensation of the baseball world came in 1961, when Babe Ruth's seasonal home-run record of 60 finally fell. Yankee outfielder Roger Maris hit 61 home runs in this season. His team also went on to win the World Series for the American League. The longtime Yankee reign as baseball's best was coming to a close, however. The careers of older stars such as Mickey Mantle were ending. The club won the series again in 1962 and lost it in 1963. The Yankees did not reach the series again until 1976, losing to National League powerhouse Cincinnati. The club won the series the two following years, 1977 and 1978.

Although the Yankee dynasty was over by the 1960s, another New York team began to rise. The New York Mets of the National League had been founded just a few years before. In their first seasons, the Mets were the joke of the league. They were known derisively as "The Amazin' Mets" because of their many errors and poor play. In 1969, the Mets stunned baseball by winning the World Series. Now they became known as "The Miracle Mets."

One of modern baseball's most thrilling moments was when Hank Aaron of the Atlanta Braves passed Babe Ruth's career home run record in 1974. Aaron broke a record that had stood for 40 years, by hitting his 715th home run that season. He would go on to hit 755 home runs in his career.

Football Chases Baseball

For all the affection Americans felt for baseball, pro football was rapidly gaining spectators. Another sports miracle came in the 1969 Super Bowl and stimulated broad interest in the sport. The underdog New York Jets defeated the more experienced Baltimore Colts in the Super Bowl. The Jets were led by playboy quarterback Joe Namath, who had brashly predicted his team's victory. This was only the third Super Bowl, which matched the champions of the two leagues. The two leagues merged as the National Football League in 1970. The Pittsburgh Steelers and Dallas Cowboys were the best clubs in pro football during this era. Pittsburgh won the Super Bowl all four times it played. Dallas also played four times in the championship, winning twice.

Television coverage of pro games on Sunday and Monday, and college games on Saturday, brought the game to the entire nation. The top college teams were led by Alabama, declared national champion six times in these decades. Texas, Notre Dame, Southern California, and Nebraska were also ranked number one several times each.

TV Boosts Basketball

Professional basketball struggled through the early 1960s. Attendance at National Basketball Association (NBA) games was relatively low, and television coverage was mainly on local stations. The NBA gained popularity in the mid-1960s, as games became higher-scoring and superstars caught the public's fancy. Television audiences saw mighty duels between centers Wilt Chamberlain of the Warriors (from San Francisco and later Philadelphia) and the Boston Celtics' Bill Russell. With the popularity of the New York Knicks in the late 1960s, national media coverage increased. Dramatic Knick performances in playoffs helped bring the pro game a wider television following. The Knicks were often matched against the Celtics in crucial games. The Celtics were the leading team of the era, with eleven league championships.

Wilt Chamberlain
(Library of Congress)

Thanks to increased television coverage, the college game also gained more followers every season. By the 1970s, college basketball's two major national tournaments—the NIT and NCAA—attracted a solid audience. UCLA was the most exciting college team of this time, wining nine of ten NCAA championships between 1964–1974.

Scholastic basketball was also going strong, with more than 20,000 high school teams by the mid-1970s. School basketball prepared young people to become avid spectators of pro basketball. In 1970, an estimated 125 million fans attended high-school basketball games. In a state like Indiana, where basketball was especially popular, some high-school gyms could seat more people than lived in the entire town.

Girls' and women's basketball gained ground steadily as more teams were established in high schools and colleges. Rules were changed to make girls' basketball more like boys'. For example, girls' rules had at first required six players three on each half of the court. As female athletes increased in ability, their basketball became more exciting. Eventually, there were five players on the full court, just like the boys' game. The crowds also increased. In Iowa, more than 450,000 fans attended the girls' basketball tournament during one season in the early 1970s. By then, some girls' high-school tournaments were outdrawing boys' tournaments.

Boxing's Sole Superstar

As the 1960s began, there were no great champions like Joe Louis or Rocky Marciano to capture the boxing public's imagination. Unlike the previous decades, few young people were interested in boxing. The sport was suffering from a negative image. It was considered corrupt, its fighters manipulated by a handful of promoters. Fighters who did not cooperate with the promoters often never got a chance to face top competition. Then a young Olympic heavyweight champion burst into the limelight.

Heavyweight champion Cassius Clay announcing his decision to change his name to Muhammad Ali to honor his conversion to Islam. He is holding a book by Nation of Islam leader Elijah Muhammad.
(Library of Congress)

Cassius Clay had won the 1960 Olympics light heavyweight division. He was a handsome, fast-talking personality. Yet he was little-known until 1964, when he got the chance to fight world heavyweight boxing champion Sonny Liston. Clay won the fight, then soon announced he was becoming a Black Muslim. He changed his name to Muhammad Ali. Ali defended his title successfully in the ring, but lost it over a controversy. He refused to be drafted into the military, declaring himself a conscientious objector—against war on moral grounds. Ali protested the Vietnam War and refused to serve. Boxing authorities stripped him of his title in 1967. Ali was arrested and sentenced to five years in prison. In 1971, the case went to the Supreme Court, which reversed the decision.

Ali recaptured his heavyweight title in 1974, defeating George Foreman in Zaire. Ali lost the title to Leon Spinks in 1978, then took it back a few months later. He was the first heavyweight to win the title three times.

Soccer's Youthful Following

The first major professional soccer league in America appeared in the 1960s. The North American Soccer League (NASL), featuring mainly foreign players, struggled during its first seasons. Unable to win much television coverage, the league seemed unable to last very long. Soccer needed a boost. The United States national team had not sparked any excitement since 1950, the last time it qualified for the World Cup.

Everything changed for American soccer in 1975, when the world's greatest player arrived. Pélé of Brazil was at the end of his career, but he was known and loved by almost all soccer fans. He joined the New York Cosmos of the NASL, attracting the attention of millions of Americans and of the media. For three years, Pélé shared his passion for the game with the United States. Increased television coverage and commercial backing made the NASL able to acquire additional great players. A few NASL clubs, such as the Cosmos, became world-class teams. At the same time, youth soccer exploded. More than 77,000 fans packed Giants Stadium in New Jersey for Pélé's last game in the United States.

The first girls' youth soccer teams had appeared by the early 1970s. Girls' high-school soccer benefited from the Congress's Title IX legislation, which required equal sports opportunities for girls. By the end of the era, girls' scholastic soccer was on its way. After high-school graduation, girls wanted to keep playing competitively. This prompted more colleges to create women's teams. Although there was no international-level soccer for women, the foundation was laid for American women's soccer to become the best in the world.

Celebrating a Birthday

A young boy, dressed as Uncle Sam and joined by a young girl, rides a parade float on Independence Day, 1976. (Library of Congress)

On July 4, 1976, the United States celebrated its 200th anniversary with a nationwide Bicentennial Celebration. America made the most of the occasion. For months leading up to the nation's birthday there were special events, parades, performances, and commemorations. It was a welcome period of recovery after the misery of the Vietnam War. All Americans, celebrating together and entertaining one another, could feel happy once more.

Chapter Nine

Fashions and Fads

A young man sports a large "afro" hairdo in his high school prom photograph. (CORBIS) Bride Jacqueline Kennedy, with future president John F. Kennedy to her left, at the couple's wedding. Throughout the 1960s and 1970s, Mrs. Kennedy (who later became Mrs. Onassis) was one of the eras top style and fashion trendsetters. (Library of Congress)

The 70 million teenagers coming of age in the 1960s dominated American culture. Their ideas and tastes remained the most important influences on fashion, style, and crazes right through the 1970s.

This era opened with short hairstyles for men and tall, teased beehive styles for women. Millions of aerosol cans of hairspray were sold to keep women's hair in these elaborate styles. By the era's end, many men and women wore their hair long and loose. Hairspray lost popularity among all but the most carefully dressed.

Clothing styles had many influences—from The Beatles and the "Mods" to the folk singer in blue jeans. Eventually, styles merged until almost any fashion was acceptable. The spirit of self-expression reigned in these decades. Creativity was the rule of the day.

Early in the era, young and stylish First Lady Jacqueline Kennedy was the dominant trendsetter among women. She continued to influence style even after her husband's assassination and her remarriage. As time went by, celebrities of older generations still had influence, but tastes were more free and easy.

Fads and crazes included pet rocks and computer games. A few, like Pop Art, set the stage for an even more volatile future to come.

Trend-setting Celebrities

In 1961, the nation's women had a refined and lovely role model: First Lady Jacqueline Kennedy. The new president's wife, like him, was wealthy, young, and well-educated and exuded well-bred charm. Soon, people referred to her as "Jackie." They celebrated the "Jackie Kennedy look," which featured a subtle bouffant hairstyle and simple A-line suits and dresses, well-fitted at the top and tapered slightly at the skirt. Sometimes, she wore a simple matching pillbox hat. Women everywhere bought patterns to make copies of her clothes or purchased knock-offs in department stores. Stores soon were sold out of the "bonnet" hair dryers that helped give Jackie her distinctive look.

The First Lady herself designed her elegant white inaugural gown with a silver-threaded bodice and matching silk cape. It was made for her at a New York department store. Mrs. Kennedy spoke French and admired French culture, but she chose Italian American Oleg Cassini as her official designer. Cassini turned out many of the A-line and sheath dresses for which she became famous. After President Kennedy was killed, and she married Greek shipping magnate Aristotle Onassis, fans simply referred to her as "Jackie O." Her large-lensed dark glasses became her new signature, and millions copied them, too.

Besides Jackie, there were several other role models. One was French sex bomb Brigitte Bardot with her red-dyed beehive hair. Another was dark-haired Italian actress Sophia Loren. A third was actress Elizabeth Taylor, in her Cleopatra costume. American women tried to copy the look make-up artists had given Taylor in her blockbuster film, *Cleopatra*. Throughout the 1960s, Taylor, Loren, and Kennedy were models for many American women.

Mods, Minis, and Twiggy

The "Mod Look" arrived from England's fashion center, Carnaby Street. Mod was sleekly tailored fashion, often close cut and featuring bell-bottomed pants. Colors were bright and contemporary, often taking advantage of new "Op Art" fabrics. "Optical" art had bizarre, dizzying effects. Stripes and slashes and stars in contrasting colors dazzled the eyes and seemed to be in motion. In 1966, miniskirts were added to the Mod look.

Skirts had never been much higher than the knee. Now they were at mid-thigh and rising. Miniskirts at first were usually worn with tights. Then, in direct response to miniskirts, pantyhose were developed. (Prior to this women wore two separate stockings held up by a girdle or a belt.)

Among the novel fads of this time were paper jewelry, paper dresses, and transparent vinyl dresses. Pantsuits also came in. Many fads did not last, but pantyhose and pant suits endured. So did "granny" eyeglasses—small-framed spectacles in the nineteenth-century style.

Granny glasses, outsized glasses, and miniskirts were put to good use by the young English "supermodel," Twiggy. In 1967, "The Twiggy Look" featured short, straight hair, and accentuated eyes. She looked like a preadolescent street waif. The following year, Twiggy and Mod seemed to merge in the newest fashion: "unisex" clothing. Designed for both males and females, unisex did not accentuate any one part of the body. Past clothing designs drew attention to a women's breasts or legs. Unisex garbed the wearer in what appeared to be a sleek, one-piece overall.

During the 1960s, miniskirts, worn with tights, became popular. This dress was created by designer Yves Saint Laurent. (Dover Publications)

From One Extreme to Another

Young Jane Fonda took her own share of the limelight with a far different look. Fonda won fame with her futuristic adventure film, *Barbarella*. She had performed in slinky, black tights, sculpted body armor, and calf-high boots.

By the close of the 1960s, a less showy female style had developed. It had to do with practicality and youthful beauty. "That young New York Look" was pictured as a woman walking home from work along a Manhattan sidewalk. She had long, brunette hair, below the shoulder, and wore a lacy white blouse. Her legs seemed longer because of her short skirt and sandals. Sunglasses were perched casually on her head, a carrying bag slung over one shoulder.

While changing styles and fashions were attracting most women, one growing segment was not going along. For them, being unfashionable was a fashion statement of its own.

In the early 1960s, many high-school students who planned to go to college had a look that was termed "collegiate." They might wear their hair either short or long, but they let it fall naturally. They seldom used hair spray and a minimum of makeup. They favored colorful, cotton Madras plaid blouses, skirts, or slacks known for their subtle fading, and loafers with low heels. As the 1960s progressed, many young women became "hippies" in reaction to what they considered an overly materialistic society. Many moved into communes where everything was shared. They began to wear overalls and shapeless dresses called shifts. Their hair was long and carelessly styled, and they abandoned make-up.

Bandanna kerchiefs were popular, and some made of tie-dyed fabrics that were cut and sewn for clothing. On their feet were sandals or "Earth Shoes." Earth Shoes had wide, comfortable toes and heels that were lower than the toes. They were said to be better for the posture than normal footwear. By the 1970s, surplus military apparel was a favorite, especially jackets. One "high style" that came out of the hippie movement was the "midi-skirt" of the early 1970s. Designers promoted the midi as a stylish replacement for the outmoded miniskirt.

Another social movement, sometimes called women's liberation or simply the women's movement, influenced how women dressed. In the 1970s, many women engaged in "consciousness raising," in which they discussed how their behavior was shaped by a culture in which men were dominant. They rejected clothing that emphasized feminine attributes. This often included underwear like bras and girdles. Many stopped shaving their leg and underarm hair.

Women who followed an alternative lifestyle often moved to the country. They dressed plainly, for gardening and for raising a family. They liked ankle-length, calico "granny" dresses in the style of the Old West frontier. And of course, blue jeans. Jeans that had survived for years were sentimental favorites. They were soft and faded, which only came of age and wearing. Usually, they were also frayed. Favorite jeans often were decorated with sewn-on patches and hand embroidery. They were cherished, even when they did not fit anymore.

Most women returned to the mainstream by the 1980s. Still, many continued to have little to do with fashion trends.

Jeans and the Flamboyant 1970s

Still, some women cared a lot about what men thought and dressed to attract them. Some trendsetters of the 1970s were celebrities like singer Barbra Streisand, actress Raquel Welch, and singer Diana Ross. Jane Fonda caused an enormous uproar when she visited North Vietnam during its war with South Vietnam and the United States. Many male and female fans deserted the woman who had been the sex symbol of her generation.

In 1971, "hot pants" came in, making once casual "short-shorts" into high fashion. Blue denim, formerly used mainly in jeans, became a favorite designer fabric. Now it was tailored into contemporary, hip-hugging styles that appealed to the most in-vogue woman. Jeans were widely popular, though they had changed. They were no longer of heavy fabric meant to endure hard use. There were now "designer jeans," and they were "pre-washed" and "pre-faded." There was no need for years of use to give them softness. Further, some jeans came "pre-frayed," as if they had been worn for years. There soon was a trend of decorating jeans, as hippies had done.

In the early 1970s, high fashion turned to the movie-star idols of the 1930s for ideas. The look borrowed from that time featured heavy makeup and "hot lips." Exaggerated lipstick, the glossier the better, was said to recreate the "bright lips of yesterday." Whether or not this was really a return to the past, lustrous lipstick came into vogue.

The media termed another creation "uppity shoes"—platforms. Introduced in 1972, platform shoes had extremely high heels and thick soles that lifted the wearer six or more inches off the ground. They were usually made of plastic and considered "splendidly flamboyant" and fun. Platforms were instant best-sellers, but did have one drawback: hospitals reported increased rates of injury from falls, especially to the feet and ankles.

Pierced ears became popular with American women in the 1970s. Until then, most had worn earrings that clipped or screwed on. Few older women chose to pierce their ears. Through the late 1970s, it was still a major decision for young women to have their ears pierced.

At the end of the decade there was a brief but enthusiastic fashion trend for women wearing men's-style clothing. It was inspired by the 1977 movie *Annie Hall*. Diane Keaton's character,

The clothing worn by actress Diane Keaton in the movie *Annie Hall* **created a fashion trend. Hall is seen here with co-star Woody Allen.** (CORBIS)

Annie Hall, suavely wore men's hats, coat jackets, neckties, and baggy pants. More traditional women wore skirts along with men's-style shirts and ties.

Haircuts and Hairstyles

How people wore their hair became a major symbol of their politics and social attitudes. By the 1970s, much about a person was identifiable in the hairstyle.

The early-1960s collegiate boys—those going to college—parted their hair on one side and let it be longer. They used little hair tonic, eventually none at all. Their hair was wavy and natural. Other young men grew their hair slightly longer and combed it back, often to a "ducktail." To keep it in place, they used oil, which earned them the nickname "greasers."

The influence of The Beatles changed many boys' hairstyles when the group took America by storm on their 1964 tour. At that time The Beatles wore their hair "longish." It hung down in a way that earned them the nickname "moptops." Many boys copied them, combing their hair forward and letting it grow much longer.

Girls' hair had been mainly in flips, bouffants, or pony tails. By 1963, many girls their hair in bouffants or beehives, well sprayed to keep it in place. As the decade progressed, many collegiate males and females adopted hippie styles. They let their hair grow much longer. In some cases, it would not be cut for years.

Many fashionable women followed the Twiggy look after 1967. They kept their hair short. This style was often favored by professional women and secretaries. It soon would develop into the popular "shag cut," longer in the back and short on the fronts and sides. In the mid-1970s, women's hair was either very short or long and lanky. Later in the decade, long braids became popular. The style was inspired by teenage supermodel Brooke Shields.

The Hair Statement

By the 1970s, adult hairstyles had become distinctive and well-established. Most conservative males still wore crew cuts or short hair, parted on one side. Moderates wore their hair longer, but well groomed and parted at the side. Liberals wore it even longer, sometimes to the shoulders, and parted down the middle. Usually, long hair on men was tied into a ponytail or held with a headband, Apache style.

African Americans of both genders often allowed their hair to grow long and full, in an "Afro." Past generations had tended to straighten their hair to eliminate its natural curliness. Now, Afros symbolized black pride and the theme "Black is Beautiful." As with long hair on whites, the Afro declared that its wearer was determined to be an individual and would not blindly copy mainstream culture.

During World War II and throughout the 1950s, American men were clean-shaven. Now even businessmen might grow a

The hairstyles of musicians Billy Preston (LEFT) **and former Beatle George Harrison** (CENTER) **contrast greatly with that of President Gerald Ford** (RIGHT). (CORBIS)

beard or at least a mustache and sideburns. The style had begun with hippies and antiwar protesters, but it spread eventually to the broader population.

Hairstyles became so significant that by 1970 the hit Broadway musical *Hair* was being performed all around the world. Set in New York City, the show portrayed a group of hippies struggling to make sense of their world. One of the male leads trusted only people with long hair. The show was so influential that six touring companies were performing in the United States at the same time.

In time, many conservative men were letting their hair grow long. A new type of barber appeared, able to style long hair. "The blow-dried look" came in, with every hair kept perfectly in place.

A large portion of veterans from the Vietnam War wore their hair long. This was in part an expression of solidarity with the antiwar movement. Few of these men were interested in flower power or hippie lifestyles, however. They generally pulled their hair tightly back into a ponytail.

Men's Fashions and Influences

The two main 1960s styles, "greaser" and "collegiate," also had definite clothing. Greasers were tough guys who wore leather jackets and tight-fitting "muscle-shirts." They also wore shirts

Handcrafting for Fun and Profit

Handicrafts of all kinds became popular with young people in the mid-1960s. For decades, a few members of the older generation had been attending arts and crafts classes and learning basic crafts skills. Among the most popular were pottery, jewelry-making, and macrame—a type of weaving with rope. It had been mainly married women who took, and taught, these crafts classes. Then, in the 1960s, the younger generation wanted to understand how things were made. How was yarn and fabric created? How could pottery be designed to be both artistic and functional? How did candles come to be? Woodworking took on great appeal for both men and women.

A man works on a handmade dulicmer. (CORBIS)

Young people found crafts to be an enjoyable outlet for their creativity. Also, they felt they could appreciate things better by learning to make them instead of just buying them in the store. Progressive colleges such as Antioch in Yellow Springs, Ohio, gave students the opportunity to include crafts as part of their formal studies. Students who were majoring in English could also be found in stained-glass studios.

There was much personal satisfaction to be found in making things that also could be used in the home. This might be a mug, a hand weaving, or a leather belt. By the 1970s, millions of Americans were learning various crafts. Many were taking formal classes, given in community centers and in schools. Others were teaching themselves and joining new regional arts and crafts associations. Several times a year, these associations held public sales.

Their members now could earn an income from their work and meet potential buyers. Professionalism in crafts rose to new heights. The American consumer acquired a newfound taste for high-quality handmade items.

Learning to work with various mediums, such as metal, wood, glass, or plaster, often led to skillful works of sculpture. In this way, the crafts became linked to the "fine" arts—painting, sculpture, and photography. One of the most demanding crafts was instrument-making. A new generation of craftspeople learned how to make guitars, dulcimers, and wooden flutes. In time, the line between crafts and fine arts was blurred. The best handcrafted work compared favorably with the most skillful works of fine arts. For most Americans interested in crafts, the real pleasure was in learning and crafting rather than selling their work. From early school years to senior citizen groups, interest in crafts became an important and well-established part of American daily life.

with large, curled collars, called "high-rolls." Their slacks were slim-legged, tapering at the bottom. They wore black socks and sharp-pointed shoes.

The "collegiate look" was plaid, Madras cotton shirts, with button-down collars. The slacks were often tan; later, blue jeans were popular. In the early 1960s, collegiate shoes were "penny-loafers," with a slot in the front to slip in a penny. Later, collegiates went sockless, in loafers or sneakers.

Most men wore ties for proper occasions. In the early 1960s, ties were narrow and narrower, with greaser ties the narrowest of all.

Elvis and the rock and roll stars appealed most to the greasers, while the folk singers Kingston Trio and Peter, Paul, and Mary appealed to collegiates. Then The Beatles appeared and won them all over. In the late 1960s, The Beatles were "Mod" in lavender suits, striped bell bottoms, and ankle-high shoes. By then, many collegiates had gone down the alternative-lifestyle road. They wore jeans and collarless peasant shirts. Their musical tastes was as much folk music, progressive jazz, or the Rolling Stones as it was The Beatles.

In the 1970s, the mainstream men's fashion world brought out bright colors, double-breasted sports jackets, and polyester pants suits. Turtlenecks and India-style "Nehru" jackets without collars were in vogue. By the end of the decade, ties were four or five inches wide. They came in swirls of colors and patterns. Many men still wore well-tailored suits, but now the pants were flared in bell-bottoms. "Leisure suits" worn with turtle necks instead of ties became a fashion for businessmen who wanted to be stylish and comfortable at the same time. Blue jeans no longer were a statement of rebellion.

Art with and without a Message

A celebrity who had a following among creative young people was Andy Warhol. He won acclaim in the early 1960s for his paintings of ordinary things, such as soup can labels. The critics called it "Pop Art." This term referred to art influenced by "popular culture." Warhol painted silk-screen portraits of film stars in wild colors. He also stacked up empty boxes, and this was called sculpture. Whatever Warhol did, including radical film making, brought critical acclaim. The art world was changed up by

A concert poster for the Grateful Dead, a popular rock band from San Francisco.
(private collection)

Warhol's originality and boldness, and many young artists tried to imitate his style.

Poster art came in during the 1960s. Every young person decorated walls and doors with posters of all sizes and varieties. They pictured rock stars and movie stars and sometimes rebels, such as actor James Dean and Ché Guevéra, a slain Latin American revolutionary. Most posters were reproductions of original art.

Among the most popular were brightly colored images of wizards and mandalas by Peter Max. Many memorable youth-culture images of the 1960s were created by Max. He said his work was meant "to carry irresistible vibrations of love." Max's kaleidoscopic colors and "day-glo" stars caught the attention of the advertising industry. Scores of companies used his images on their products. Max designs were perfect for appealing to the youth market. Merchandisers put them on everything from panty hose and pillow cases to tea bags and stationery. In the 1960s, more than $250 million worth of goods were sold with Peter Max artwork on them.

Playthings as Fads

From the moment they were introduced by the Mattel toy company in 1959, Barbie dolls were a runaway success. Barbie was, perhaps, the era's most sought-after toy. Every little girl had to have one—and all the gear, clothing, and accessories that went with it. Competing toy manufacturer Hasbro soon brought out a rival to Barbie: G.I. Joe. At 12 inches tall, G.I. Joe was the first mass-marketed "action figure" for boys. Like Barbie, Joe had all sorts of accessories. He was a soldier who needed equipment: helmets and rifles, radios and jeeps. G.I. Joe was a strong second to Barbie.

Another toy hit of the 1960s were slot cars. These were racing cars that followed a slotted track at high speeds. Slot cars were so popular that they passed electric trains in annual sales.

Skateboarding and turtle-racing were fads by 1975. A year later came video games and the absorbing board game, "Dungeons and Dragons." The 1970s had "mood rings" that changed colors according to the wearer's emotions. Also, there was an endless appetite for collecting miniature characters from the hit movie, *Star Wars*. Even "pet rocks" captured people's imagination. These painted rocks were collected, given as gifts, and treated like pets and friends.

Th first computer games came in at the end of the 1970s. They would become the rage of the 1980s.

On the Brink of a New World

The baby boomers came of age in the 1960s and 1970s. They played and performed and demonstrated their way through these decades. In the end, they were grown up, and many were parents themselves. They had new responsibilities as adults and citizens. Most outrageous behavior, fads, and fashions were long past by 1980. Their youthful energy, imagination, and spirit of individualism had laid the groundwork for the next decade. The 1980s would be more conservative, more responsible.

Bibliography

Ahearn, Robert. *Decades of Cold War: American Heritage Illustrated History of the United States, Volume 16*. New York: Choice Publishing, 1988.

Bowen, Ezra, ed. *This Fabulous Century: Volume V, 1960–1970*. New York: Time-Life Books, 1991.

——————————. *This Fabulous Century: Volume IV 1970–1980*. New York: Time-Life Books, 1991.

Ciment, James. *The Young People's History of the United States*. New York: Barnes and Noble Books, 1998.

Derks, Scott. *Working Americans, 1880–1999*. Lakeville, CT: Greyhouse Publishing, 2000.

Groner, Alex. *The History of American Business and Industry*. New York: American Heritage, 1972.

Harvey, Edmund H. *Our Glorious Century*. Pleasantville, NY: Reader's Digest Association, 2000.

Mintz, Steven and Susan Kellogg. *Domestic Revolutions: A Social History of American Family Life*. New York: The Free Press, 1988.

Weiss, Suzanne E. *The American Story: Who, What, When, Where and Why of Our Nation's Heritage*. Pleasantville, NY: Reader's Digest Association, 2000.

Index

Note: Page numbers in *italics* refer to illustrations.